A. Lynch.

SOCIAL CARE Practice

SOCIAL CARE Practice

JANET MILLER

Hodder & Stoughton
A MEMBER OF THE HODDER HEADLINE GROUP

Orders: please contact Bookpoint Ltd, 39 Milton Park, Abingdon, Oxon OX14 4TD.
Telephone: (44) 01235 400414, Fax: (44) 01235 400454. Lines are open from 9.00–6.00,
Monday to Saturday, with a 24 hour message answering service.
Email address: orders@bookpoint.co.uk

British Library Cataloguing in Publication Data

Miller, Janet
  Social care practice
  1. Social service
  I. Title
  362

ISBN 0 340 65516X

First published 1996
Impression number   12 11 10 9 8 7 6 5
Year   2004 2003 2002 2001 2000

Cover photography by Dan Addelman; Joanne O'Brien/Format; Crispin Hughes/Photofusion;
Judy Harrison/Format; John Almond/Guide Dogs for the Blind–Holidays

Typeset by Wearset, Boldon, Tyne and Wear.
Printed in Great Britain for Hodder & Stoughton Educational, a division of Hodder Headline Plc,
338 Euston Road, London NW1 3BH by J. W. Arrowsmith Ltd., Bristol.

To my family

Contents

List of Figures   x

Acknowledgements   xi

Introduction   1

1   Social care – what is it?   4
    Service users   6
    Dependency   8
    Empathy   9
    Institutionalisation   9
    Normalisation   11
    Keyworking   12
    Suggestions for further reading   14

2   Values and principles – their application to social care practice   15
    Values   16
    Principles   17
    Suggestions for further reading   22

3   Anti-discriminatory practice (written by Susan Gibb)   24
    Definitions   25
    Forms of discrimination   26
    Benefits of promoting anti-discriminatory practice   28
    Achieving good practice   29
    Ensuring good practice continues   32
    Examples of good practice   33
    Important points about anti-discriminatory practice   34
    Suggestions for further reading   34

4   Community care   35
    Community care as a concept   35
    Key factors which have influenced policy and provision   37
    The National Health Service and Community Care Act 1990   38
    Examples of community care   40
    Suggestions for further reading   44

5   Communication, relationships and counselling   45
    What is communication?   45

Verbal, non-verbal and symbolic communication 46
Examples of good communication 48
Important points about good communication 51
Relationships 52
Being responsive 54
Counselling 55
Suggestions for further reading 61

6 **Assessment and care planning** 62
Needs-led and service-led approaches 62
Full and partial assessments 63
Assessment as part of a model of care 64
Important points about assessment 64
Tools of assessment 66
Care planning and care agreements 72
Important points about care planning 73
Care planning and resources 73
Full and partial care plans 74
Suggestions for further reading 76

7 **Implementing care plans** 77
Behavioural work 77
Task-centred work 84
Developing networks 85
Advocacy 91
Working with groups 93
Groups and groupings 93
Group stages 94
Advantages of working with groups 96
Suggestions for further reading 99

8 **The care environment approach** 100
Physical environment 101
Organisational environment 102
The care maintenance and therapeutic environment 107
Community environment 111
Suggestions for further reading 112

9 **Collaborative work** 113
Skills of collaborative work 113
Teamwork 116
Team meetings 117
Advantages of teamwork 120
Co-working 120

Collaboration outside the agency   122
The host organisation   122
Other agencies   123
The local community   123
Multi-disciplinary work   124
Suggestions for further reading   126

10 Writing things down – records and reports   127
Types of recording and report writing   128
Essential principles of recording and report writing   128
Functions of recording and report writing   129
Recording systems   132
Legislation   132
Suggestions for further reading   133

11 Evaluating and ending   134
Evaluating your work and yourself   134
Supervision as a means of evaluating practice   134
Endings – how you finish things off, deal with goodbyes and with loss 137
And finally . . .   140

Afterword   143
Communication   143
Tomorrow   145
The Social Carer   147

Glossary   149

References   153

Index   157

List of figures

Figure 4.1   The core and cluster project   41
Figure 5.1   The Oomph factor – contributed by Ellen Lancaster   47
Figure 6.1   The tree of a model of care practice   65
Figure 6.2   A personal history flowchart   69
Figure 7.1   The ABC Model   80
Figure 7.2   Jim's network at Fernlea   88
Figure 7.3   Jim's network after six months at Fernlea   89
Figure 7.4   Ted's network in the core and cluster project   90
Figure 9.1   Collaboration   114
Figure 9.2   The service user and the multi-disciplinary team   125

Acknowledgements

Thanks are due to many people who contributed generously of their thoughts and their time. I am grateful to my colleagues in the Health and Social Care Section of Cardonald College, Glasgow and to the many service users, social care workers, students, managers and friends who gave help and encouragement. Particular thanks go to Ellen Lancaster for her Oomph and support, to Philomena McDonald, Angela McMahon, Frances Toland, Julian Crispin, Jim Davidson, Theresa McLaughlin, Donna McCall, Fiona Campbell, Karen Motherwell, Joan Keery, to Mary Cartledge for the graphics, to Ann Morrison, Jean Tennant, Cathy Vencta, Leo Chuen and Lily Johnston at Crookfur Cottage Homes, Susan Gibb for Chapter 3, Carol Sallows for her thoughts on counselling, to HNC Social Care students and the following people who read and commented upon chapters of the book: Sue Bates, Chris Bush, Doris Graham, Sadie Hollis and Marie Sommerville. Thanks also to Donna Hazely, Jacqui Harvey and Margaret Miller for secretarial support and diagrams, and to Elisabeth Tribe at Hodder & Stoughton whose comments were always helpful. There were many conversations which I had along the way and I'm sorry that I haven't mentioned everyone's name who played a part ... but thank you anyway.

Janet Miller
May 1996

Notes on contributors

Susan Gibb	Lecturer in social care at Cardonald College, Glasgow.
Carol Sallows	Counsellor/social worker with The Women's Counselling and Resource Service, Glasgow City Council Department of Social Work.
Jim Davidson	Unit Manager (Community Care), Renfrewshire.
Ellen Lancaster	Lecturer in social care at Cardonald College, Glasgow.
Julian Crispin	Social care worker with Sense in Scotland.

Introduction

One of the main aims of this book is to encourage practising and training social care workers to think about their practice and to ask themselves 'is this the very best I can do?' It encourages a constant questioning and stresses the importance of the apparently small everyday gesture, as well as the big innovative idea.

Originally, the book began as a way of structuring material for the HNC Unit, Social Care Practice and Skills, but has broadened its scope to be of relevance to anyone working or training to work in a social care setting, particularly at HNC/HND level or at level III of an NVQ or SVQ. The task of social care is a difficult and challenging one, not to be underestimated or undervalued. It is a front-line task which makes a difference in fundamental aspects of life for often very vulnerable people. It requires a value and skill base which can come only from training. This book begins to tackle some of the training requirements. At least as many questions are posed as are answered and one major aim, if all else fails, is to make you think. Often there are no absolute answers, no one right way of doing things, and certainly one person, even with a lot of help, cannot present a comprehensive work which will cover every situation or setting. However, you can be encouraged to think about your work and how best to do things with this particular individual or group.

Throughout the book I have tried to give examples to illustrate practice. Examples are based upon true situations but have been fictionalised in order to maintain confidentiality. Occasionally, where both the service user and the social care worker have given their permission, I have used real names and real situations – some service users stressed how they wished their own experiences to be of value to other people. An attempt has been made to follow a logical sequence and to include most of the issues relevant to social care workers. There will inevitably be gaps and comment on the content of the book is welcomed. A good deal of literature examines the everyday practical skills and tasks usually covered at national certificate level but not dealt with here, and this book can be read against a background of such guides as Thomson, (1995) and Rogers, (1990).

I have used the term 'social care worker' to refer to anyone working in the social care field. In practice, such workers have many different titles. At times in the text, where it has seemed appropriate for the sake of brevity or where another author is quoted, the terms 'social carer', 'care worker', 'worker' or 'helper' appear. The term 'service user' is examined more fully in Chapter 1.

The chapters of the book are as follows. Chapter 1 is a preliminary chapter which looks at what social care is, how social care workers see their task and what service users would like from social care workers. Concepts of dependency, empathy, institutionalisation, normalisation and keyworker are introduced and an exercise invites you to envisage admission to a social care agency and what this might be like. Chapter 2 establishes the value base

1

through a discussion of values and principles. These provide the foundation upon which the practice of social care is built. There is an emphasis upon the values of respect for the worth and dignity of every individual and of according social justice and promoting social welfare. A set of principles is derived from the key values to include promoting acceptance, maintaining privacy, maintaining confidentiality, promoting the right to protection from abuse, exploitation and violence, promoting choice, empowerment and risk taking, and promoting fulfilment and potential. In Chapter 3, Susan Gibb develops some ideas and promotes thinking about anti-discriminatory practice.

No book about social care would be complete without an examination of community care which is permeating practice and affecting the ways in which social care is delivered. This is the subject of Chapter 4. The chapter looks at community care as a concept, factors which have influenced community care policy and provision, community care in legislation – especially the National Health Service and Community Care Act 1990 – and community care in practice. Chapter 5 examines communication, relationships and counselling skills. Communicating and forming and maintaining relationships are at the heart of social care and are the most basic skills needed in all care settings. The meaning of and different kinds of communication are examined: verbal, non-verbal and symbolic. The essence of 'good' communication is illustrated through the use of example. Carol Sallows, a counsellor and social worker, contributed most of the ensuing section on counselling skills.

Chapter 6 concentrates on the specific role of the social care worker in the assessment/care planning process. It emphasises how knowledge of the content and process of assessment and care planning can enable social care workers to participate fully alongside the service user and other professional workers. The implementation of plans is introduced in Chapter 7 and is continued in Chapter 8, which specifically concentrates upon the care environment not only as the background to everything social carers do but also as an integral part of the caring process.

Collaborative work is the subject of Chapter 9. There is emphasis upon the skills of communication and relationships, flexibility, negotiation, working in partnership and evaluation. Teamwork receives particular emphasis and consideration is also given to co-working, collaboration with other agencies, collaboration with the local community and to multi-disciplinary work. Chapter 10 looks at records and reports as vital elements of communication and of the social care worker's task. The essential principles and functions of recording and report writing are examined, together with recording systems and legislation which relates to recording and report writing. There are some useful exercises for those who find this aspect of the work difficult or challenging.

Finally, Chapter 11 tackles evaluation, the last element of the model of care practice, and endings, including departures. The value base is re-emphasised at the end of the book as a way of bringing the reader back to thinking about what is of fundamental importance.

Although the book has not arisen from a specific piece of research, many people were talked to during the writing of it – service users, social care workers, managers, teachers, friends – who were all helpful and did not hesitate to state their views. Literature relating to social care and social work, and the publications and recommendations of the Social Care Association, have all been helpful. For the views expressed and for the content of the book, except the two sections written by other authors, I take full responsibility. They are not necessarily the views of any organisation to which I belong.

1 | Social care – what is it?

The underlying purpose of all social care is to improve the quality of people's lives.

Social Care Association, *The Social Care Task: Improving the Quality of Life*, March 1993.

Social care is changing – perhaps that is the only certain thing about it. At one time 'social care' and 'group care' meant almost the same things, but now it is difficult to attempt a useful definition. As group care settings change their nature to become incorporated into an overall policy of community care, opportunities are presented for caring for people in all sorts of new ways, with traditional concepts undergoing radical revision.

Exercise 1

What do you think social care is? Write down a few suggestions to help clarify your ideas.

A group of social care workers, when asked what they thought social care was, came up with a list of suggestions, which is by no means an exhaustive or 'correct' one but does give some idea of the diversity of things which social care might include. Many of these points will be expanded upon during the course of the book.

The group made the following suggestions about what social care involves:

- caring for people and helping them to improve their lives

- performing caring tasks, enabling the fulfilment of needs, helping with personal hygiene e.g. assisting people to the toilet, equipping people with skills, training

- emotional support/listening

- maintaining and promoting independence by giving choices, individual attention, encouragement and a sense of responsibility e.g. enabling service users to deal with their own medication

- enabling service users to maintain a sense of self respect

- allowing risk taking

- family work

- protecting the individual/family/society

- promoting social interaction e.g. in day centres

- the joint process of assessment/care planning/implementing/reviewing *with* rather than *for* the service user/family

- empowerment and advocacy

4

- setting realistic boundaries and limits, and helping to develop self discipline

This may be what care workers see as their task, but is this what people want from them? I discussed this with a group of service users: Jean, Cathy, Leo and Lily, at Crookfur Cottage Homes in Glasgow. This is what they said about 'good' care workers:

- it's their kindness and they take care

- they make you feel you're wanted and that nothing is a problem

- there's a loving feeling between the care workers and ourselves

- we like being taken out by them on the bus

- they try to accommodate us if we don't like what is presented

- they know their job

- we like them to be outgoing and cheerful

Ann Wheal (1994) looked at what young people wanted from their social care workers. They wanted them to:

- share information with the young person about his or her rights under the law and make sure that the young person fully understands any legal order affecting him or her

- acknowledge differences, whether due to racial origin, language, religion or culture; respect and support young people and challenge discrimination

- provide opportunities for young people to make choices and to learn about making decisions; involve them in planning

- remember that in dealing with parent(s), young people are also partners in the decision making and may need support in making their views known

- help young people to participate in their reviews

- prepare young people for independence

- share information about pocket money and allowances

- support young people in making a complaint

- help young people develop other relationships and other partnerships

- advocate for young people in obtaining equal opportunity in education

- recognise and support young people in distress

- recognise that the best partner may be the key residential worker or foster carer

Although this research was confined to young people, many of these points can equally be applied to any service user group.

Exercise 2

Go to your own group and ask the service users what they want from their care workers – you may be surprised. Appreciate that for some people communication, especially verbal communication, is difficult and you therefore have to do this exercise within the abilities of the service users. It may also be necessary to enlist the help of others involved in their care (relatives, friends, other carers) to interpret some of their wishes. As far as possible, however, this exercise should be done with the users themselves to ensure that their views are accurately presented. With the information gained as a beginning it can be added to, altered, expanded upon and developed as knowledge and understanding increases.

Service users

Throughout the book the term 'service user' has been employed to refer to people who use social care services. This is the term which is currently most in evidence in social care and social work literature, and is the term adopted by the Social Care Association. It has come to prominence as a term without stigma or the sometimes patronising overtones of 'client' or 'resident'. Since both 'client' and 'resident' are still fairly common currency, they have occasionally crept into this book, especially in quotes from other works. I am conscious that the term 'service user' is not embraced with overwhelming enthusiasm by everyone. It is a little cumbersome but with use gains in warmth. It certainly does force upon the worker a vocabulary which concentrates more upon the people being worked with as users of a service and not just as passive recipients or residents in one particular place, or 'owned' by the provider of the service.

Who are service users?

Service users might be:

- Joe, aged 87, who lives alone and has had several falls recently. He is at present in a residential home for a period of respite care and assessment. He may return home in a few weeks with a package of care to enable him to maintain as much independence as possible, or he and the care team may find an alternative solution which is satisfactory to him and meets his needs.

- John, aged 14, whose parents experienced many problems and are no longer able to care for him. He is living in a children's home at the moment but hopes to go back to live with his father in the near future.

- Emma, aged 26, who has learning difficulties and attends a day centre five days a week. She lives in a 10-resident hostel run by the local authority social services department.

- Donald, aged 42, who has profound learning difficulties and attends a training centre on weekdays but goes home at night where he is supported by his parents with help from a home support worker.

- Anna, aged 93, who was admitted to a residential home following a spell in hospital. She has decided to make the home her permanent residence since she feels unable to cope alone again.

Exercise 3

After reading these short descriptions write down or discuss what you think the social care task is likely to be with these service users. You can add more detail to this as you progress through the book or after you have read the example below.

Case example – Joe

In order to illustrate the kind of suggestions which could be made, I will use Joe as an example. What is the social care worker likely to be doing in relation to Joe? First of all, Joe has been admitted, probably on a temporary basis, to residential care. The social care worker must initially be sensitive to what this means to Joe. It may be a regular occurrence for the worker but it is something which happens to Joe very rarely, probably only once. It is a major event in his life – it might be a crisis. He will need a lot of understanding, someone who will listen to anything he has to say; he will appreciate a warm, friendly welcome, perhaps a cup of tea, introductions to staff and residents or maybe some time alone. Put yourself in Joe's shoes and imagine how you might feel – empathise with him.

Joe may also have some physical needs which he is unable to meet without some help. He may need assistance to go to the toilet (not 'toileting', an impersonal expression which should be abolished from every care worker's vocabulary) or to take a bath. Any assistance he needs should be given in a way which emphasises his own worth as a human being and which allows him to retain his dignity, and should rest firmly upon a social care value base. Joe has been admitted not only for respite care but also for assessment. The social carer should therefore be competent to participate in this assessment process and recognise its significance to Joe and his future.

Joe might be a little, or even very, challenging and the care worker may have to deal with aggressive outbursts, balance Joe's needs and those of others in the home, and understand why Joe may be behaving in such a way without condoning his behaviour or labelling him as difficult. In addition to these tasks, the care worker needs to recognise the importance of enabling Joe to make as many decisions as he is able and wishes to make himself. This requires an understanding of empowerment, of the principle of independence and the way in which, unless care workers are alert to the dangers, any kind of care environment can inadvertently act as a means of disempowering and institutionalising a service user. Some of the terms used here, for instance 'empowerment' and 'institutionalisation', are clarified as the book proceeds and in the Glossary.

Thus the care worker's task, initially, in relation to Joe may be summarised as follows:

- sensitivity to his needs
- warmth and a welcoming approach
- possibly some physical assistance
- skills of assessment
- the ability to deal with difficult behaviour
- enabling and empowering Joe to maximise his potential

The task may extend beyond these to other things. There may also be:

- additional keyworker tasks to perform
- considerable communication about all sorts of issues both with Joe and many others involved in his care
- collaboration with outside agencies
- discussion between the care worker and Joe using a particular approach to enable him to act more independently in some area of his life

The care worker's task is a complex one, a balancing act. In the words of the Social Care Association:

> *A characteristic of good social care practice is the ability to meet physical needs at the same time as respecting the feelings of others and addressing social, intellectual, emotional and cultural needs, responding to strong emotions and dealing with difficulties in behaviour and relationships. (Social Care Association,* The Social Care Task, *March 1993.)*

This sums up very well the many facets of the social care worker's task and just how many things the good social care worker has to take into account.

Now that Joe has been considered, you can return to the exercise above. Examine particularly the social carer's task in relation to service users.

At this point it seems useful to examine some of the other concepts which occur time and again in discussions about social care practice, so that they can be used without further discussion later in the text. These concepts are:

- dependency

- empathy

- institutionalisation

- normalisation

- keyworker

An understanding of these, together with a firm grasp of the social care value base and communication skills, will establish a foundation for discussion of a model of care. This is based upon assessment, care planning, implementation and evaluation within a framework of genuine respect and concern for the well-being of the service user, and through caring relationships committed to providing the best possible quality of life.

Dependency

One thing many people do not like about accepting any kind of help is that it involves being dependent upon others in some areas of their lives. A whole range of emotions is evoked by the initial feeling of the need to accept help, and I think that it is very important that the care worker acknowledges that these feelings may exist and then minimises any negative aspects of them by promoting self worth.

Negative feelings

Some of the negative feelings may be:

8

- a sense of loss, anger, betrayal, fear or insecurity

- a feeling of being punished or of having done something wrong

- a sense of imprisonment, restriction or lack of privacy

- a loss of identity or continuity

- a feeling of embarrassment or rejection

- money worries

- resistance to change

- worries about a partner and other family members

- concern about privileges (for example being allowed out or allowed to smoke)

- concern about house and pets

- a feeling that this is the slippery slope downwards

- feelings of failure and guilt, emptiness or numbness

Positive feelings

Mingled with the negatives may also be positives. Service users told of their relief, of looking forward to companionship, security, lack of worries and a sense of wonderment. One of the things which I hope that this book will bring out is that care and caring should be positive experiences. They can only be positive experiences if negative feelings can be dealt with, preferably at the very beginning. One of the most important ways of dealing with the negatives is

communication. Good communication is the key to good social care and receives much more attention later in the book. Here, its importance is emphasised. One of the most important parts of communication is listening. The social care worker has to be a good, attentive listener. One young person in Wheal (1994) stated that 'A good carer is someone who sits down and listens to you and discusses things with you'.

Empathy

One of the most valuable assets when working with people is a willingness to try to feel what it must be like to be the other person. What is it like to need help and what must it feel like? This attempt to put oneself in another person's shoes is called empathy. Of course, it is impossible to know exactly how someone else feels. The statement 'I know how you feel' can only be a false one; but it is the attempt and effort which matters. This concept receives further development in Chapter 5.

Institutionalisation

The importance of institutionalisation lies in the efforts which social care workers need to make to avoid it, both for service users and for themselves. Institutionalisation is a state of being which often results from residence in long-term institutional care, although it does not necessarily arise as a result of living in an institution; nor is it a feature resulting from residence only in large, total institutions such as long-stay psychiatric hospitals. It can occur in people who spend even quite short stays in care unless efforts are made to counter its causes and effects.

What is 'institutionalisation?'

Erving Goffman, in his book *Asylums* (1961), has presented one of the best known expositions of the concept and I will concentrate here on his analysis. Goffman was particularly interested in total institutions, of which he identified five broad groupings. The terminology is his and may seem somewhat dated. The groupings are:

- places which care for people such as the old, the blind and orphans

- places for people seen as a threat to society e.g. mentally ill people, people suffering from TB etc.

- places which protect people from perceived dangers e.g. prisons, prisoner of war camps and concentration camps

- places which allow limited access and have a functional use e.g. barracks, ships and boarding schools

- places designed as 'retreats' from the world e.g. monasteries and convents

One of the main features of these institutions, according to Goffman, is that a person's self concept is changed and 'taken over' by the institution. In the outside world a person's self concept is built up and maintained through his or her social world, including relationships with family, friends, work colleagues etc. Once inside a total institution, however, this world is to a large extent lost. The processes of admission and institutional life contribute to the breakdown of a person's former self concept and individuality is denied. This breaking down of self is sometimes referred to as the 'mortification of self' and some things which contribute to this are as follows:

- role loss

- undressing and wearing regimented clothing

- hair cutting

- fingerprinting

- expected co-operation and/or obedience

- deprivation of clothing, name and/or possessions

- expected verbal responses

- humiliation and/or ill-treatment

- keeping of personal details on record open to others

- regimentation which means deprivation of personal decisions and daily routine

- work organisation often disguised as 'rehabilitation'

It does not even take all of these for a condition labelled 'institutional neurosis' to set in. This has the following characteristics:

- apathy

- lack of initiative

- loss of interest

- submissiveness

- lack of interest in the future

- inability to make practical plans

- deterioration in personal habits

- acceptance that things will go on as they are

- occasional aggressive outbursts

- characteristic posture

In some understaffed, unimaginative homes for elderly people these characteristics can be observed – not back in 1970, but in the present day. The characteristics which seemed most to contribute to this pathetic state of affairs were:

- few, if any, efforts to maintain contact with the outside world

- no activities, a lot of empty time and enforced idleness

- a large social distance between staff and service users, with staff in uniforms behaving in an authoritarian way

- working to a medical model

- hardly any prospect of ever going out of the establishment, either temporarily or permanently

- a lack of respect for the dignity of individuals, demonstrated through belittling expressions and no regard for privacy

- an almost total preoccupation among staff with the practical aspects of the job – meals, baths, cups of tea etc. – with no thought given to possible improvements in the quality of life for service users

- staff immensely interested in their own affairs and talking to one another as if the service users were not there

Normalisation

Normalisation is central to the philosophy of this book. It goes several steps further than deinstitutionalisation in emphasising that not only should people who have impairments or disabilities or who become service users for whatever reason be enabled to avoid institutionalisation, but they should also be empowered to lead socially valued and fulfilling lives in ways which are also socially valued, if they want to. This means the pursuit of lives which are as normal as possible, keeping the needs of the individual at the forefront.

'Normal' is a difficult term to use. What is normal after all? Is anyone leading a normal life? 'Normal' is not a particular way of life, it just means having the freedom to exercise the choices and to make the decisions which are the right of every citizen and human being.

Not only does it mean not being institutionalised but also being able to participate with equal rights in society including in education, housing, leisure and work. It is a very sane concept which puts decision making firmly back where it belongs, as far as possible in the hands of the service user.

I recently walked through the door of a home for elderly people and heard the care worker saying to a group of 'residents', 'Come on, girls and boys'. She said it in a kindly way, but this is what normalisation is out to combat. It is about treating adults as adults with rights and dignity. It is an opportunity to do away with patronisation, hypocrisy and segregation.

It aims for maximum integration, and sees segregation as reinforcing stigma and disadvantage.

The ideas about normalisation were developed by Wolfensberger (1972) and have been taken up by many writers since then. One of the best explanations which I have read is contained in *Beyond Community Care*, edited by Shulamit Ramon, in which she emphasises the necessity for attitudinal change:

> *In particular the approach challenges the perception of people with disabilities as inferior to those without them, as passive recipients of charity and professional wisdom, as having nothing to give but only to take, as needing care but unable to care for themselves or for others. In so doing, the accepted divide between professionals and users, between the givers and those in need is threatened. (Ramon, 1991, p 26.)*

David Brandon, in the same book, pursues the subject and looks at how training often increases rather than decreases the divide between worker and service user. He sees in normalisation 'a framework for the conscious adoption of a new set of values, to provide more coherency between what we say and what we do'. His is a wonderful article full of irreverence for the accepted ways of doing things and full of genuine respect for people, whoever they are. He pursues five major themes as contributing to normalisation: good relationships; maximising choices; effective participation; personal development; and greater mixing.

Some policies have been adopted which keep normalisation at the forefront. The Canadian state of Alberta, for example, has adopted a policy of integration for people with learning difficulties. Almost all specialised agencies have been abolished and provision is made through mainstream agencies available to all citizens. Emphasis is laid upon all citizens having equal rights of access to buildings, transport, education and all other services. A colleague who worked there for a while felt that the policy was working well and had the support of the media, of policy makers and the general population. It had been brought about initially through the enormous efforts of relatives and supporters to promote the rights of every citizen.

On a smaller scale, some agencies have tried to reverse staff/service user roles by enabling service users to be equal members on the management committee, and to answer the door and be responsible for decision making when visitors arrive. What is needed is a humanitarian approach, so that we do not hide behind qualifications or positions, but show ourselves willing to share the job with the users of services; so that we do not always think we know best, but are able to learn from service users about what they would like and how they would like it, and to provide the circumstances for this to be possible through our attitudes and through such practical measures as improving access and setting up opportunities for real communication to take place.

Keyworking

'Keyworking', as defined by the Social Care Association, is:

> *. . . a system for providing individualised care through named persons. A keyworker is the person who has responsibility and accountability for the care of the service user and for decisions relating to their situation. (Social Care Association, 1991.)*

12

The keyworker enables the service user to know that there is at least one person, in addition to the head of the care agency, to whom he or she can turn for support who has understanding of needs, wishes and rights. This is a form of empowerment and should serve to prevent feelings of being lost in a group, unable to turn to anyone who might understand. The keyworker role provides an opportunity for real communication in a relationship which can be built up over a period of time, and this relationship is something which can determine a service user's attitude to a period in care or attendance at a day centre.

There can be keyworker involvement in preparation for attendance or residence at a social care agency. The keyworker can be involved in introducing the service user, getting to know him or her before admission and facilitating admission to make it as pleasant and non-traumatic as possible. In this way admission can be seen as a bridge to cross over rather than a wall to climb with something unknown and hidden on the other side. The 'matching' of keyworkers to service users is very important. It is not always possible for people to choose whom they want for a keyworker, but as far as possible service users can be given a choice and the opportunity to change if the relationship proves unsatisfactory.

The keyworker role is used in different ways in different settings. There is no one right way of developing the task, although essentially it is a partnership between worker and service user. One thing which agencies can do to maximise the benefit to be gained from the keyworker role is to discuss how it can be best developed. Such discussion can be with both service users and staff members in joint meetings, in staff meetings and informally. The nature of the role can be written down, evaluated and changed as experience alters its perception. There needs to be agreement about what the task involves so that it does not become a vague and meaningless idea. Also, since the keyworker is a member of a team, other team members will need to be aware of what keyworkers and service users are doing and the keywork will have to be viewed in terms of the work of the team as a whole.

Keyworking is not without its problems. As keyworkers, staff are answerable to both the service user and to management, and this may give rise to conflict. Perhaps sometimes the service user needs an ally outside the agency, someone without any agency responsibilities who will act as an advocate solely on his or her behalf. Staff are not on duty all the time and some form of co-keyworking may be worked out in order that service users are ensured of a keyworker on duty for a maximum amount of time. Ideas about co-keyworking are further developed in Chapter 9.

Any power differential which exists between the service user and the worker should be minimised rather than maximised through the keyworker role. Keyworkers act as part of inter-dependent teams and will often be working with many service users at the same time. It is essential that what is keyworking is distinguished from what is not. There is also a need to ensure that keyworking does not become a kind of favouritism, but a positive force for good. I do not think all of these potential problems are in any sense an excuse for abandoning a role which has great possibilities.

To summarise, among the things which a keyworker may be doing in partnership with the service user are:

- developing a dependable relationship

- co-ordinating care and co-ordinating the care plan

- advocacy and empowerment

- just being there as a reliable, approachable, dependable person – an ally in difficult times

- maintaining, exploring, encouraging and expanding the service user's network of links with family, friends and other agencies

- monitoring care to ensure that it is as good as it can be

Exercise 4

Envisage your admission to a social care agency. Try to do this in terms of somewhere you know well or where you work e.g. a residential unit, a day centre or a housing project. What do you think your feelings might be? What do you think would be the most helpful things a social care worker could do to make the experience as pleasant as it possibly could be?

Suggestions for further reading

- Craig, M. (1979) *Blessings*. London: Hodder & Stoughton.

  Written with great feeling and literary skill by the mother of two children with learning disabilities. Many students find this compulsive reading, giving them new perspectives and understanding of the problems which parents, relatives and friends face.

- Ramon, S. (ed.) (1991) *Beyond Community Care*. London: Macmillan in association with Mind Publications.

  A challenging, lively book, particularly helpful in looking at normalisation.

- Rogers, J. (1990) *Caring for People, Help at the Frontline*. Milton Keynes: Open University.

  A warmly written, practical and relatively short introduction to caring.

- Thomson, H. (et al.) (1995) *Health and Social Care for Advanced GNVQ*, 2nd edn. London: Hodder & Stoughton.

  This is a comprehensive and useful guide with 452 pages of information about equal opportunities, legislation, human development and much more.

2 | Values and principles – their application to social care practice

Young people said they were not being listened to, were patronised, refused help, and their confidences were betrayed.

MARCHANT, *COMMUNITY CARE*, 22 DECEMBER 1994.

A residential care home in Strathclyde is to be closed after a confidential report . . . revealed a catalogue of neglect.

'NEGLECT FORCES HOME CLOSURE', *COMMUNITY CARE*, 22 DECEMBER 1994.

Social care practice in a multi-cultural, multi-racial society can to a large extent make the difference between whether the lives of service users are miserable or meaningful, hurtful or happy, public or private, with choice or chosen for them. The values and principles used to guide practice are the foundation upon which this practice is built. Behind much poor practice which is criticised by service users, the press, the courts and others, there is often a lack of knowledge, understanding and practice of values and principles essential to good social care. Such a value base can make the difference between good and poor practice. If social care workers respected service users, their privacy and confidentiality, we would not hear that many care leavers feel that no one cares for them ('A Word from the Street', *Community Care*, December 1994).

Perhaps Glenrosa Home, where residents were said to be treated like human livestock, need never have been closed down if owners and care workers had been secure in their practice of a value base which had respect for the worth and dignity of service users as fundamental to practice (*Community Care*, 22 December 1994).

The necessity for a value base with a set of guiding principles has been outlined many times (for example Wagner (1988); Social Care Association (1994); Centre for Policy on Ageing (1996); and Residential Forum (1996)), but because it cannot be assumed and because care workers should be constantly reassessing their own practice in terms of such a value base, a suggested set of guiding values and principles is outlined here. There is nothing startlingly new about these values and principles. What I have tried to do is to present them in a way which is clearly stated and which is compatible with syllabuses in social care such as HNC, NVQ and SVQ.

The terms 'value' and 'principle' are widely used in the literature of social care, and it may be useful at this point to distinguish between them in a theoretical way in order to avoid confusion. Books about social care and social work abound with accounts of principles and accounts of values, often not distinguishing one from another, if indeed they can be distinguished. Principles are derived from values, often overlap with them, are sometimes called by the same name and are sometimes treated as if they are totally unrelated to values. No wonder that workers become confused. A value, according to the *Oxford English Dictionary*, is that which is desirable or worthy for its own sake; a thing or quality having intrinsic worth. A principle, however, may be defined as a rule of conduct, especially right conduct. Principles are the practical manifestation of values and rest upon them, which is why I have discussed them in detail. They relate directly to the everyday work of the social care worker. The principles rest upon the following two core values at the heart of social care, or indeed any work which involves helping people.

Values

Respect for the worth and dignity of every individual

This means that every person has the right to be regarded as having worth simply because that person is a person. This involves individualisation, showing respect for that particular person, whoever he or she may be, and in whatever state of mind.

It includes an effort to empathise with the service user and to encourage self esteem where this may have been lost.

According social justice and promoting the social welfare of every individual

Social justice refers to the right to fair and correct treatment in society, especially ensuring legal rights. Social welfare refers to ensuring that well-being is maximised, including the right to welfare services and benefits. The care worker should be committed to both of these ends and should be familiar with sources of information and services to promote them.

Exercise 1

Before discussing the principles derived from these two core values, it may be useful to look at your response to the following statements. Please answer 'yes', 'no' or 'don't mind' to the following questions:

Do you value for yourself or a friend:

1) Being accepted by the people you go out with for the person you are, even though you recognise that you may have shortcomings, may hold different views from them, or have done something in the past of which they would probably disapprove?

2) Choosing whether to share your bedroom and with whom?

3) Being able to talk to someone in the knowledge that what you say will not be passed on to others?

4) Being able to lock your door and refuse permission to others to enter your room?

5) Feeling safe with the people you live with?

6) Being free to marry and bring up children if you want to?

7) Being able to vote?

8) Being encouraged to make the best of your abilities?

9) Having the opportunity to pursue qualifications or further education if you want to?

10) Feeling part of the world in which you live?

All of these questions relate to the principles of social care. When you have finished reading this chapter go back to these questions and ask yourself to which principle each question refers. If you have answered 'yes' to these questions, then it is likely that these things are also valued by service users. Do you promote these principles? Do you think that they matter?

These principles are now examined one by one so that their meaning can be clarified in practical terms. It should be recognised, however, that there is a great deal of overlap between one principle and another. Separating them clarifies their meanings but does not mean that they stand in isolation.

Principles

Promoting acceptance

This means taking people as they are without judging them. It does not condone or ignore behaviour but implies that whatever a person is or has done he or she is entitled to our help. Many of the people with whom social carers work have been judged by others, for one reason or another, to be difficult or undeserving. It is important that social care workers do not carry over these assumptions into their practice or apply inappropriate labels. One student who had preconceived ideas about the group of people called 'elderly' felt that she had nothing to give such a group. Another student who is working with long-term prisoners is able to get past the label of 'prisoner' to accept the individual and so is able to work fruitfully towards rehabilitation and fulfilment.

Maintaining privacy

If we respect people then it follows that their right to privacy should be preserved. Some invasions of privacy were mentioned in discussion with students. In one children's home teenagers were required always to keep their room doors open. Is this privacy? Another student recognised her own invasion of the privacy of another. She knocked on Mrs Smith's door and then walked straight in without waiting for a reply. Mrs Smith was changing her clothes and was embarrassed, though not visibly annoyed, by the student's entrance. The student felt awful because she realised that she had breached an important practice principle. She also realised that she was following what was common practice in the home in which she was working, and was able to bring this matter up in supervision. Only in this way can long-standing poor practice be changed.

Maintaining confidentiality

This is really an extension of the privacy principle, since it is maintaining the right to privacy of information. One way of looking at this is to emphasise that confidentiality is not about secrecy. It is about the appropriateness of sharing, transmitting or storing information about a service user where a number of competing factors may influence decisions about information use. There are several ways in which this principle can be maintained in practice:

- by keeping all records under lock and key when not in use

- by gaining permission from the service user if you want information to be shared

- by restricting access to records to the service user and 'approved' others

- by keeping confidences (though there are some limitations here imposed by law and agency policy – these should always be explained)

- by not talking about service users or their carers behind their backs or to others who are not members of the care team

A conversation overheard on a bus was brought back to me by a student. Two care workers were discussing a service user, known to the student, in a derogatory and judgemental way. This disregarded both the principle of confidentiality and the principle of acceptance. A similar example concerned a student whose mother was being discussed by two members of staff in the home in which she was on placement. They were talking about the relatives of the service user, judging them to be uncaring because they had allowed their mother to be placed in a home. The student who overheard this discussion was extremely distressed and felt betrayed by her colleagues. They knew nothing of her mother's choice or the stressful circumstances which had surrounded her admission to care. Again, they breached confidentiality in unnecessary discussion and were judgemental of people about whom they knew little or nothing.

Promoting the right to protection from abuse, exploitation, violence, neglect or any kind of harm

Abuse, exploitation, violence, neglect or harm may be among the reasons for someone needing care. Abuse may be mental, physical, sexual, medical or financial and includes both exploitation and neglect, though for emphasis these are mentioned separately.

Misuse of power lies at the basis of abuse. The least that people can expect is that they should be protected from this while in the care of others. This has not always been and still is not, unfortunately, the case. Examples taken from 1994 issues of the magazine *Community Care*, include:

- several private homes closed because of a catalogue of neglect

- a resident of a home suffered horrendous bedsores and subsequently died

- residents treated as 'human livestock'

- a children's home worker sacked following allegations of assault on a teenage boy

- allegations of rape and excessive restraint at a school for children with severe learning difficulties

- a care officer imprisoned for the sexual abuse of children in his care

Would we have noticed? Would we have said anything? These things should never happen and if care workers of the future can acquire accepted social care principles, can be encouraged to train, are carefully selected and can be encouraged to analyse their practice, they will not happen in the future. It is the duty of every social care worker to ensure that service users receive protection not only from threats from the outside world but also from within the care setting from other service users and from workers. Any suspicions should never be left unsaid. Social care workers carry ultimate responsibility for the protection of those in their care, and they should be familiar with their agency procedures for the protection of service users.

Promoting choice, empowerment and risk taking

These three principles are inextricably linked with one another and for this reason are discussed together.

CHOICE

Choice means giving different options, real options; it does not mean, for instance, offering a choice between community care and residential care when there are insufficient community services to fulfil need. The choice must be based upon real options and the service user should have, wherever possible, the opportunity to select independently from these choices. Choice is not only about choosing on a large scale, choice about big decisions which affect life in a major way, but is also about small-scale choice, choosing this item of food or clothing rather than that one.

EMPOWERMENT

Empowerment means enabling people to take control of their lives, having the power to make decisions and choices. It goes beyond providing choices in that it means putting the individual in a position where these choices can be made, not just at a practical level but at a psychological level. It is a very important principle in caring since many service users may have spent many years in a situation of powerlessness. The process of institutionalisation is a prime example of a process which disempowers people and deprives them of their ability to make decisions.

For example, John, who had been in long-term hospital care, was astonished to find that in the hostel in which he went to live he had the choice to close the toilet door if he wanted to – even to lock it – and he did not have to ask permission to do so. He also had the choice to go outside or to stay in. Taking these decisions, however, was not as easy as making a simple choice because John had forgotten, or had never learned, how to make choices.

So empowerment is sometimes also about unlearning helplessness and learning at a thinking level that choice and decision making are not only a possibility but that, in the end, they provide a reward in terms of fulfilment and satisfaction with life. Empowerment may be a very slow process, where the care worker is placed in an educational role of showing what is possible and offering encouragement and support to people who have not been used to exercising power in any area of their lives. Once the process is under way it is a continuing one, as Stevenson and Parsloe have pointed out:

Empowerment is an evolving process and has no clear end point, which may explain the reluctance with which it is sometimes regarded. (Stevenson and Parsloe, 1993.)

RISK TAKING

Choice and empowerment necessarily embody an element of risk. It is impossible to give people choice and power without this, and reluctance to take risks on the part of care workers may actually infringe the rights of service users. Crookfur Cottage Homes in Glasgow have incorporated this into their 'Principles of Care for Residents in the Home':

Responsible risk taking is regarded as normal. Excessive paternalism and concern with safety may lead to infringements of personal rights. Those who are competent to judge the risk to themselves are free to make their own decisions so long as they do not threaten the safety of others.

Choice, empowerment and risk taking are important to everyone. A behavioural support team in Berkshire (*Nursing Times*, 10 March 1989) works with people with learning difficulties, physical disabilities and severe challenging behaviour. It states that in providing choice:

Carers need to be innovative, to explore, for example the sensory responses of people with profound physical disabilities and to consider tactile responses and eye tracking movements as techniques to identify personal choices and build on decisions.

Here are some useful quotes about choice, empowerment and risk taking:

Daily within the centre there is a choice of activities which the service users have the opportunity to participate in. However if someone does not wish to join any of these activities they cannot be forced to do so. Service users should also be consulted as to what activities take place within the centre. It is after all their centre, not the staff's. (FC, social care worker.)

On reception into care and where feasible both young people and parents/guardians should be given certain choices. To do this successfully admissions should be on a planned basis. This would allow young people and parents to be given information about all units available, therefore enabling choice right from reception. This rarely happens and young people are more usually received on an emergency basis and placed whether appropriately or not in any vacancy. (JK, social care worker.)

People should be encouraged as far as possible to make choices. This helps to teach independence and encourages acceptable risk taking. Being able to make choices about one's life can be a sign of maturity. One service user has recently chosen to become involved in a project to help her move out of the unit, eventually to a home of her own. Making that choice has made her feel good about herself. She'll be supported in her choice, and would have been whatever she decided. (KM, social care worker.)

Promoting fulfilment and potential

Service users have a right to expect more than basic care from social care workers. They should also be enabled to lead rich, fulfilling lives and to reach their maximum potential. This may be through the provision of educational opportunities, a choice of activities, outings, and the provision of an environment which is conducive to creative and leisure activity. Service users should also have access to advice and guidance about available opportunities for training, education and other facilities in the community. Social care workers have a duty to look beyond the immediate environment of the service user and the care setting in assessing how to gain maximum benefit from that setting. This requires an ability and willingness to find out about local resources, to encourage participation in and by the local community and to be active in improving care when this is possible.

When I asked a group of social care students how they would promote fulfilment and potential this is what they came up with:

• empower the service user

• promote choice, acceptance and independence

• respect the worth and dignity of every individual

• practise individualisation and avoid labelling people as drug users or residents – see the person first.

So far this illustrates how far they see all of the principles as being related to one another, in that one cannot be practised without bringing in all of the others. They also advocated:

• the avoidance of boring routines

• encouraging service user participation in all aspects of life

• encouraging people to open up a bit

• the need for advice, information, education and community resources

• the need for social care workers to gain knowledge of what is available in the wider community.

All of this will go towards building up self esteem and will promote fulfilment and potential. You can formulate your own interpretation of this principle within the context in which you work.

Promoting anti-discriminatory practice

This principle is placed last because extensive consideration is thought to be required in view of its tremendous importance and emphasis in practice. A separate chapter is devoted to it (Chapter 3) and here I only briefly touch upon its meaning.

Discrimination can be defined as negative or less favourable treatment of someone because of an actual or perceived difference. It is based upon prejudice and involves stigmatising others. Stigma implies a negative reaction which has no logical or moral basis. Anti-discriminatory practice necessitates:

1) Demonstrating an awareness of both individual and institutional discrimination on the grounds of nationality, sex, age, disability and religion; also an awareness that the service user's position may also sometimes be a potential source of discrimination.

2) Ethnically and culturally sensitive practice.

3) Working towards counteracting the impact of discrimination and challenging discriminatory words and acts.

Exercise 2

This exercise gives you an opportunity to think about the value base in terms of your own practice, involving the completion of a chart based upon one week of practice. Complete the chart below in terms of values and principles and their meaning (first column), how each one was achieved (second column), and what could be done, if anything, to improve practice in relation to each value or principle (third column). It should be a magnified version of the chart set out below.

Suggestions for further reading

- Centre for Policy on Ageing (1996) *A Better Home Life*. London: Centre for Policy on Ageing.

  An updated version of *Home Life* (1984), which became something of a practice bible. This new version presents a revised code of practice for the continuing care of older people.

- *Community Care* magazine. Haywards Heath: Reid Business Publishing.

  A weekly magazine for practising care workers which has lots of examples of good practice, discussion of the value base, news and jobs.

- The Residential Forum (1996) *Creating a Home from Home*. Available from Surbiton: Social Care Association.

  This publication provides a comprehensive guide to standards in care homes, focusing on the people who live in them and the promotion of their quality of life. Dame Gillian Wagner states in the foreword, 'Open any page and under any subject heading the guide has something relevant, practical and balanced to say'.

- Social Care Association publications available from: Social Care Association, 23A Victoria Road, Surbiton, Surrey KT6 4JZ.

  A lot of very useful leaflets, booklets and books for the social care worker, including the 1994 *Code of Practice for Social Care*.

- Stevenson, O. and Parsloe, P. (1993) *Community Care and Empowerment*. York: Joseph Rowntree Foundation in association with Community Care.

  An excellent discussion of the empowerment concept; short and readable.

- Wagner, G. (1988) *Residential Care, A Positive Choice*. London: HMSO.

Values and principles, their meaning	How these are achieved	Suggested improvements

The work of working parties is often rather boring to read but this one is not. It gives a very full discussion of choice, and although the title refers to residential care the work is of relevance to anyone involved in social care. There are many examples of both good and bad practice ... and the shades of grey in between.

3 | Anti-discriminatory practice

Anti-discriminatory practice challenges people's values and their taken-for-granted assumptions in constructing their own sense of reality. Such a challenge can prove very threatening and destabilising . . . The focus needs to be on educating and convincing, not bullying.

THOMPSON, 1993, P 154.

Discrimination is something which all of us have experienced at some time in our lives – it is not an external phenomenon which just happens to other people. Stereotypes and labels may have been assigned to you by others which have resulted in a limiting of your opportunities, actual harm, embarrassment or anger. Discrimination may be:

- your authority as a worker questioned because you are young and/or female

- guarded behaviour or concern about your motives for applying for a certain job because you are homosexual

- being refused accommodation because of your colour

It would be useful to look at your own experience of discrimination before going any further, so that you can relate the rest of the points in this chapter to your own circumstances, as well as considering the issues for other groups and individuals.

Exercise 1

Make a list of any occasion on which you have felt discriminated against or excluded from a group. Consider the different stages of your life, jobs you have had or leisure interests you have pursued. Then consider the things you would have liked to do and think about the reasons why you did not follow them up. Was actual or potential discrimination one of the reasons you did not achieve what you wanted? For example, did you feel you would not be accepted, or fit in, or get the right kind of support or help?

As you make this list, you will begin to remember some of the ways you felt at the time – perhaps you were angry, embarrassed, hurt, violent or upset – and some of the ways it affected your behaviour – perhaps you were unable to complete a task, unable to perform to your best ability, or you never went back to a place again/walked home a certain route/applied for a type of job. Make a note of the ways in which you were affected. It will be useful to refer back to later in this chapter when we consider how service users may respond to discriminatory practice.

24

This chapter is concerned with linking your own experiences to the wider picture of discrimination, acknowledging that although most people have experienced discrimination of some kind, there are certain individuals and groups for whom discrimination is a major influence and daily occurrence in their lives. So, while we look at your own thoughts, feelings and behaviour, we will place this in the context of social policy and culturally acceptable behaviour which clearly results in negative treatment of specific individuals and groups such as disabled people, women, black people, elderly people and homosexuals. This list is clearly not definitive, but attempting to name particular groups raises an important issue. Neil Thompson, in his book *Anti-Discriminatory Practice* (1993), discusses the concept of 'multiple oppressions'. He argues that it is not always helpful to see each group as an individual entity because 'race, class, gender and so on are . . . not separate processes; they occur simultaneously and affect people in combination. They are related dimensions of our complex existence rather than discrete entities'. Rather than pigeonhole people according to one factor then, it is important that any anti-discriminatory approach looks at the whole person and acknowledges the totality of his or her experience.

As a worker therefore it is valuable to remember that 'oppression and discrimination are multi-faceted phenomena and so it is important to gain an understanding of both the common themes across areas and the key differences between them' (Thompson, 1993) when we consider how best to improve practice.

Definitions

In order to implement anti-discriminatory practice, we need to be clear about what discriminatory practice is: negative or less favourable treatment of someone because of an actual or perceived difference. This can arise from prejudice, lack of knowledge, lack of understanding or failure to implement good practice.

Prejudice

This is a belief held by someone about another individual – or group of people – which is unfounded, negative and based on a stereotype of that person. It is a refusal to see that person as an individual with independent rights and needs, and is often based on ignorance and fear. A prejudice is a negative attitude and like all attitudes is based on an individual's background and upbringing and can be influenced by the dominant values of society.

Examples of such prejudices may be:

- women are not suitable for 'male' jobs

- black people are not capable of achieving educational results equal to those of white people

- gay people should not 'come out' in the armed forces or sports clubs as it will reduce team performance.

Lack of knowledge

This involves simply not being aware of the needs and choices of an individual or group. This might include information about:

- dietary requirements

- religious practice

- naming protocol

- rituals for death and preparing to die

- cultural differences in personal hygiene

If you as an individual, or your workplace, are not aware of these different practices and requirements, you may find yourself unable to respond appropriately to each service user's specific needs. This may lead to situations, for example, where there is not an adequate range of food to cater for all religious requirements, or where people who are HIV positive are shunned because of concern about spread of infection due to lack of knowledge about safe procedures.

Lack of understanding

This occurs when you are aware that people have traditions, rituals, needs or beliefs, but you do not accept, or acknowledge them as being important. This may be because of disinterest or disrespect, but the message is the same: the person is not seen as an individual worthy of interest or effort. In this situation, people often feel that they are 'invisible' or that their uniqueness is not being acknowledged.

Examples of this are:

- not providing books or magazines that reflect the diverse backgrounds and experience of service users

- not having publicity material or leaflets in other languages

- assuming that all service users are heterosexual and therefore not having a culture where someone would feel comfortable disclosing his or her homosexuality

Failure to implement good practice

You may be in an organisation which does have equal opportunity guidelines and trains staff to be aware of discriminatory practice, but on some occasions these may not be fully implemented. This may occur if there is staff sickness, and there are temporary workers who are not aware of the guidelines, or it may be when new members of staff or service users, who are not so committed to anti-discriminatory practice, join the organisation. These situations raise the point that promoting anti-discriminatory practice is not a static event, but needs to be addressed in a continuous way in an establishment by both staff and service users.

Forms of discrimination

Not all discriminatory practice is obvious and intentional. However, other forms of discrimination which are hidden or unconscious can be equally damaging in terms of reducing self esteem and denying opportunities, and can often be more difficult to complain about because of their nature.

Direct discrimination

This is where a person is intentionally and visibly treated less favourably than others. Based on prejudice, an individual or group is denied access or opportunities in a situation in which other people would expect to have them. Examples of this would be:

- sacking a pregnant woman

- being physically attacked because of colour or religion

- being sexually harassed

- not being offered a job because of disability

Indirect discrimination

This occurs when a requirement or condition is applied that has a disproportionately adverse impact on one group, or is impossible for one group to comply with. It is a more difficult concept to understand, but the following examples may help to illustrate the point:

- prioritising previous contacts with an area when allocating housing indirectly discriminates against incoming ethnic groups

- expecting employees to be freely available to work unplanned extra hours indirectly discriminates against anyone who is responsible for organising care for their dependants

- requiring a worker to wear a skirt for a particular post indirectly discriminates against Muslim women, who would not be able to comply with this without conflicting with their religious dress codes

It can be seen therefore that indirect discrimination can be perpetrated intentionally or unintentionally.

Unconscious discrimination

This is unintentional but nonetheless unfavourable or negative treatment of an individual or group. The use of language comes within this category. Take a minute to consider the number of terms of abuse that are based on negative images of women, elderly people etc. Many of the assumptions that we make – automatic associations of elderly people as being a burden, or equating disability with illness – are part of this 'taken for granted' form of discrimination. Since these assumptions are often based on the general stereotypes we pick up in society, people are often not aware that they are making negative comments or links until this is pointed out to them.

Institutional discrimination

This occurs when the unfavourable treatment of a group is enshrined in law or is part of the accepted practices of an organisation or society, and affects the ability of an individual or group to access the rights, rewards and resources that other groups can expect.

Examples of this would be:

- the age of consent being higher for male homosexuals than for heterosexuals

- lack of adaptations for disabled people to gain access to public buildings

People often point to the composition of Parliament, or the senior management of local authorities, to illustrate how difficult it obviously is for women, black people or people with disabilities to break through the institutional barriers within education, politics and the workplace.

An individual or an organisation therefore needs to address the issues raised at all of these levels and in all of these ways in order to claim honestly that it is attempting to promote anti-discriminatory practice. This may seem an overwhelming task, but it is not expected that these changes will happen overnight. Indeed, the most effective changes occur at a rate that allows the individual and the work group time and resources to deal with the issues and contribute to policy and practice, rather than have changes enforced from above without consultation.

Benefits of promoting anti-discriminatory practice

Many excuses and justifications are given for not having made more of an effort to challenge discriminatory practice in our own lives, or in the organisation for which we work:

- lack of interest, time, resources and staff

- irrelevance ('we don't have any Sikh service users, so we don't need to know about their customs')

- resistance to new ideas

- a feeling that this is just another phase of political correctness which will soon be overtaken by another

- lack of support from management or colleagues

- uncertainty about how best to train people on the new issues

These are all points that need to be considered in the light of your own situation and may take a lot of effort to address, but as a basic starting point, we have to realise that discriminatory practice is bad practice.

Some of the benefits of good practice are discussed below.

Good for service users

You will be unable to work within the values and principles of social care if you are not implementing anti-discriminatory practice. You will not be protecting service users from abuse, exploitation, violence, neglect or any kind of harm; you will not be promoting choice or empowerment; you will not be promoting fulfilment or maximising potential. Service users will have more access to more opportunities if you truly see them as unique individuals and do not resort to stereotypes and labels. Often service users will have had the experience of having their identities denied or ridiculed, and their self image devalued. It is important to create an environment where they feel not only tolerated, but indeed supported, respected and valued in their uniqueness.

Good for workers

If anti-discriminatory practice is implemented effectively, it will have brought a staff group together as a team to address how they may best improve their practice, acknowledging problems and agreeing on appropriate changes. As stated in *Promoting Equality in Care Practice*:

Teamwork is a source of strength and a forum for the acknowledgement, explanation and open discussion of issues that affect our ability to carry out 'good practice' in practically all social and health care situations. Workers are individuals and also members of a team. Teamwork provides the opportunities to take collective action based on consensus. This in itself gives individuals a source of support and confidence. (Waterside Education and Training, 1994.)

Teamwork and a policy of anti-discriminatory practice will have created an organisational culture where staff will feel less threatened by discrimination and harassment against themselves, and where they feel confident to tackle discriminatory behaviour in others. The concept of teamwork is further explored in Chapters 8 and 9.

It may be illegal if you discriminate

Increasingly, people are using the courts (both British and European) and industrial tribunals to uphold their rights and make complaints of unfair treatment, using legislation such as the Sex Discrimination Act 1975, the Race Relations Act 1976 and various European Union directives. Many workplaces have complaints procedures and are subject to outside scrutiny from inspection units and registration bodies. All of these groups have power to punish individuals or organisations if their work is unsatisfactory. Improving practice in response to the threat of litigation is never the best way to achieve effective change, but it does give individuals who want to initiate changes some official recourse if they encounter obstructions.

Achieving good practice

Much work can be done by individuals in an attempt to raise their personal awareness of issues, but effective change will only be achieved when this is backed up by accompanying changes at work

group and organisational levels. However, these improvements will only be maintained if there are changes at a structural level in society. There is not the space to deal with the latter issue here, so I shall look at what you can do as individuals and members of an organisation to improve practice, using the categories mentioned earlier.

Prejudice

This needs to be tackled directly in the workplace, as any improvement in anti-discriminatory practice requires an increase in self awareness among all staff and service users. People need to be encouraged to think about their own negative attitudes and how these might impact on the service users and other staff. Prejudices and stereotypes are formed over many years and cannot be expected to change overnight, but it its also true that attitudes are not static and people will reconsider their points of view in the light of new information or experience. That is why sessions aimed at challenging preconceived ideas are often effectively held in group or training sessions, where people can hear other opinions presented.

People who feel threatened in such group situations can pose a problem if they see their role in a group as being disruptive or as challenging the leader, or other people's contributions. However, good facilitation should deflate this and allow the other group members to air their views. If the person does not attempt to gain insight into his or her prejudiced views or behaviour, then the organisation should consider other avenues, such as individual supervision sessions, to deal with this.

Exercise 2

Look at how your own attitudes have been influenced. Think about your family, the country or area in which you were brought up, the people you mixed with, the papers you read, the television programmes you watched. To what extent did any of these things help influence the ideas and attitudes you have today?

To look at how attitudes can change and differ, think about yourself as a 16-year-old. In what way are your present attitudes different? What reasons made you change your view: was it meeting someone new; an experience that affected the way you look at things; the opinion of someone you respected; reading things? Advertisers and politicians are daily trying to influence our attitudes and use many of these ploys in trying to win us round. Consider how easy or difficult you have found it to change your mind about some issue in the past. It is a lot more difficult to change your attitude when you do not have acceptance for that change from those around you.

Another useful exercise is to consider how different your views are from those of your close family and friends. Is there a pressure to conform, or are differences tolerated?

group exercises to work on. Importantly, they see exercises like these as being part of a process, rather than as ends in themselves. Having one or two training sessions without any backup is not enough to help people reconsider ingrained beliefs.

Lack of knowledge

It is both an individual's and an organisation's responsibility to ensure that they are fully informed of the diversity of needs presented by service users. Individually, most of us do well to familiarise ourselves with the requirements of current service users, but as a work group or organisation, we should be addressing the issues of why certain groups or organisations do not use or seek our services. This is an example of where you can actively pursue anti-discriminatory practice. It is not just enough to say 'the service we provide is good for those who currently use it'. You also might consider whether the needs of all of your potential users are really being met elsewhere in the community or if you offer or publicise your service in a way which makes it less attractive or relevant to certain groups.

There are an increasing number of resource books which provide exercises to use in raising awareness, including: Waterside Education and Training (1994) *Promoting Equality in Care Practice*; Powell (1994) *Gender and Diversity in the Workplace*; and Oxfam UK and Ireland (1994) *The Oxfam Gender Training Manual*. All of these books take a practical approach to increasing the visibility of oppressed groups and discussing the opposition people might have to dealing with their own prejudices. They provide a great variety of case studies, worksheets and

Exercise 3

There are many ways in which you, as an individual or as part of a work group, can increase your knowledge with a view to improving your service. Which of the following would be most relevant to your organisation?:

1) Have a group brainstorm to see where you feel you could make improvements.

2) Consult national groups such as the Commission for Racial Equality, the Equal Opportunities Commission,

Stonewall or the Royal Association for Disability and Rehabilitation, for guidance or advice.

3) Consult local groups like disability or elderly forums, gay and lesbian centres, community relations councils and ex-offenders groups, for information and local contacts.

4) Seek out other local organisations which have already addressed the issue of how to make their service more accessible to all potential users.

5) Survey current users and identify potential users so that you can gain their opinions.

6) Buy or gain access to books, journals, or resource packs such as the Employment Development Group's *Equal Opportunities Directory*.

7) Encourage staff and service users to attend relevant support groups, training days or conferences on specific issues. Individuals could follow up a specific area of interest which they then feed back to the rest of the group.

Lack of understanding

Even if people increasingly have more knowledge about other group's needs, this is no guarantee that the needs will always be acknowledged or implemented. A useful way of highlighting the effects of having your differences ignored is through role play simulations. To consider for yourself how it feels to be discriminated against can often provide the platform to re-commit yourself and your organisation to promoting good practice in an active way. Good role plays enable you to think

about the consequences of having your choices denied. These role plays are not intended to be a true reflection of what it actually feels like to be a member of an oppressed group – it would be insulting to imply that. Rather, they are exercises in achieving empathy: trying to consider what it might be like in a particular situation. It would also be useful to consult the personal list of occasions on which you have felt discriminated against which you wrote at the beginning of the chapter, and refer to how you felt when people did not make an effort to understand your needs.

Exercise 4

(Adapted from an exercise originally published by the Scottish Council For Voluntary Organisations)

Imagine that you have had to move to a new country because of high unemployment in the UK. You have left many of your family behind, and have had to move into temporary accommodation while you seek something more suitable. You have taken a basic course to learn the native language but most people cannot understand what you are saying. Your children are being bullied at school and there is nowhere you can go to practise your religion. Your festivals are not acknowledged, let alone celebrated, and people find your style of dress peculiar.

Take five minutes to consider how you and your children might feel and react in these circumstances and what effects this situation is likely to have on your attitudes and behaviour. Thinking about this situation will hopefully provide a basis for discussion about the position of ethnic minorities in the UK today.

Exercise 5

This exercise needs to be done with a considerable degree of planning and forethought, but can serve the purpose of gaining information as well as insight.

Visit a place you are not familiar with, bearing in mind safety factors, and having first sought any permissions required. This may involve going to a religious ceremony of a group you do not belong to, going to a festival or a conference organised primarily for a group you are not a member of, or even attending a foreign film (without subtitles). The purpose of this is to experience temporarily the possible confusion, isolation and lack of confidence that is felt when you are in a situation which does not cater for your needs. Discuss how you felt and what might have been done to make you feel more comfortable.

Exercise 6

Bearing in mind the safety considerations, work as a group to establish situations which simulate a given state e.g. blindfold someone to simulate having a visual impairment, use earplugs to create a hearing impairment or use a wheelchair to simulate impaired mobility. The purpose of these exercises is to attempt to participate in some everyday activity – participating in a meeting, having a cup of coffee, going for a walk – and to gain a temporary insight into the types of obstacles you encounter. This exercise could be seen as patronising to the groups mentioned, but students often increase their awareness and understanding when the exercise is well organised.

In what way could your organisation or workplace become more accessible to people with these and other disabilities?

Ensuring good practice continues

Having begun to tackle issues of prejudice and discrimination and worked towards increasing individual self awareness, there are two ways of underpinning the improvements in good practice in your workplace:

- develop an appropriate equal opportunities policy

- monitor and evaluate it

The former without the latter can often mean that little effective change occurs. Without some system of monitoring and evaluating you will never be able to check whether the policy is useful, relevant and effective. A good policy helps support carers and users who want to maintain improvements and keep equal opportunities on the agenda. Blakemore and Drake (1996) have a useful discussion about the relevance and purpose of equal opportunities policies.

A good policy will arise from a consultative process with all relevant staff and service users. Huczynski and Buchanan (1991) describe how decisions made as part of a participatory process are more likely to be acted on than ones imposed in an autocratic manner. This is because it allows everyone to share their concerns and voice opinions. If organised sensitively this process will leave individuals feeling more committed, supported and informed.

The areas which may be included in any discussion about an equal opportunities policy and approach are:

1) **Definitions** – of discrimination, what groups are included in the policy?

2) **Advertising** – where will appointments be placed? What varied images of people will be used in publicity?

3) **Selection and interviewing** – who is on the interviewing panel? What type of questions are allowed? How are interviewers trained to avoid bias?

4) **Staff training** – awareness raising on issues; increasing knowledge of other groups' lifestyles; how to implement the equal opportunities policy in practice.

5) **Harassment and victimisation** – clear definitions, the procedure for complaints.

6) **Support** – what type of support is available to staff with e.g. AIDS, HIV or other chronic illnesses?

7) **Redundancy, discipline and dismissal** – monitor why people leave and check that one group is not disproportionately affected e.g. part-timers workers.

8) **Monitoring, assessing and reviewing** – mechanisms to ensure that the policy is effective and relevant; procedures for changing it if it is not.

If your workplace already has a policy, is it publicised to all new staff and service users? Is there a clear understanding of whom to go to if you have a complaint? Do all staff and service users have confidence that their complaint will be taken seriously and dealt with efficiently and confidentially? Are staff members given training to deal with implementing the policy? Is the policy monitored and reviewed regularly?

The importance of having a policy is not just that it gives clear signals to staff and service users that discrimination will be taken seriously, but that it encourages people to assess, and reassess, whether their practice fits within the policy. If there is a culture of openness and tolerance which has led to the development of the policy in the first place, then regular sessions on improving practice, whether in individual supervision sessions, staff meetings or training days, or when doing an annual review, will soon build up a solid base of good anti-discriminatory practice.

Examples of good practice

Examples of good practice abound in the social care field. Increasingly when new projects are set up, anti-discriminatory practice is an integral part of ensuring service users' individual needs are fully met. Examples of this are when smaller children's homes are established on the breakup of a larger institution. Staff are now flexible enough to encourage children to follow their own habits and lifestyles. Another example is an existing building which was converted into a multi-cultural community centre for elderly people. There are a number of activities on offer which meet the needs of the local white, African and Asian communities. Importantly, members have the choice to organise activities for a specific group of people. For example, Muslim women may want to meet in a group without men present. This is an important aspect of anti-discriminatory practice: listening to a group's needs means that the answer is not always integration with all other groups, but an opportunity to meet and socialise on their own terms.

A third example of good practice is where a project for training people on issues of sexual abuse discovered that their material was not accessible to deaf women and, in fact, deaf women had particular needs for information and training related to their situation. This project set up links with other organisations dealing with deaf women to produce new material directed specifically at this group and has met with a lot of success in doing so.

Important points about anti-discriminatory practice

Anti-discriminatory practice is a key component of providing a good service, otherwise service users' needs are not being met. There are many ways in which an individual and an organisation can address the various levels of prejudice, disinterest and lack of knowledge which exist. Increasingly, there are organisations and books which will guide and support anyone who wishes to improve his or her practice. However, there is always a question of resources. Does an agency have enough staff time or money to spend on anti-discriminatory practice when it lacks the basic facilities for service users? Some people also ask if it is really necessary to go through all these exercises and information gathering sessions. Is there a real benefit for you and your work group? The only answer to this is to repeat what has been discussed earlier: if you were the person whose needs were being ignored, or whose needs were not being catered for by a group, or who received negative treatment, what action would you want? Would you prefer social care workers and other users to show an interest in you and respect your individuality, or just more excuses as to why nothing could be done?

Anti-discriminatory practice is about making an effort to bring about change. It needs an active approach, not just meaningless guidelines. It involves social care workers and service users in looking at their own attitudes and making changes at a personal and organisational level so that everyone in the organisation feels welcomed and respected. This is not an easy task, but it is an essential one.

Suggestions for further reading

• Blakemore, K. and Drake, R. (eds.) (1996) *Understanding Equal Opportunities Policies*. London: Prentice Hall.

Discusses the background to equal opportunities policies, how they developed to help different groups of workers, and how to use them effectively, while addressing some of the criticisms levelled against them.

• Thompson, N. (1993) *Anti-discriminatory Practice*. London: Macmillan.

This looks at the historical background and theoretical base of anti-discriminatory practice. Thompson examines each of the main areas of discrimination in a social work context and discusses ways of improving practice.

• Waterside Education and Training (1994) *Promoting Equality in Care Practice*. Association for Social Care Training.

An accessible source book of exercises and worksheets on such issues as individual beliefs, choice within service delivery and promoting good practice.

4 | Community care

To the politician, community care is a useful piece of rhetoric; to the sociologist it is a stick to beat institutional care with; to the civil servant it is a cheap alternative to institutional care which can be passed to the local authorities for action or inaction; to the visionary, it is a dream of the new society in which people really do care; to social services departments it is a nightmare of heightened public expectations and inadequate resources to meet them. We are only beginning to find out what it means to the old, the chronic sick and handicapped.

JONES, BROWN AND BRADSHAW, 1978.

Utopia, paradise, a cheap alternative, an excuse, a nonsense, the exploitation of women in disguise, a revolutionary idea, a promise – community care has been described as all of these things. It is an idea, a philosophy and a policy. The idea has been around for a long time. Griffiths (1988) tells us that community care has been talked of for 30 years; even the Elizabethan poor laws of the 16th and early 17th centuries can be seen as the first steps in implementing care in the community by the community, though amendments in the 19th century when workhouses were compulsorily established on a national scale militated against the original idea. So how have things changed? What is new, or relatively so, is the implementation of specific community care legislation embodied in the National Health Service and Community Care Act 1990. Although I have purposely avoided discussion of policies and legislation specific to the UK or parts of it, this is one piece of legislation which is having a profound effect upon the ways in which both social and health care are practised, the need for care is assessed and the ways in which services are delivered. It is also affecting the ways in which people think about care. For these reasons I see it as important for social carers to understand this piece of legislation, its implications for them and the factors which have led up to it. More importantly, it is useful for care workers to have some understanding of the concept itself; the philosophy of community care rather than just the way in which it happens to have been incorporated into legislation.

Community care as a concept

The meanings of the words 'community' and 'care', and of the term 'community care' are surrounded by some controversy.

Traditionally, a community has been seen as '... an area of social living marked by

Exercise 1

Write down what you think about the word 'community', the word 'care' and the term 'community care'.

some degree of social coherence. The bases of community are locality and community sentiment' (McIver and Page, 1961). This raises questions about the relevance of locality to most people in a mobile society and the relevance of sentiment or feeling about that locality in an individualistic age. What feelings do you have about your locality? Could you rely upon it if you needed help? Who would provide that help? Do you think of your locality as a community?

Willmott and Young (1962) made the point that where kinship and locality coincide the kind of community which McIver was defining was more likely to exist than when relatives lived in different localities and found it difficult to see each other on a regular basis. They emphasised the importance of kinship in a sense of community. Barclay (1982) moved away from the emphasis on just locality or kinship to provide a broader definition of community. He defines community as:

... a network or networks of informal relationships between people connected with each other by kinship, common interests, geographical proximity, friendship, occupation, or giving and receiving of services – or various combinations of these. (Barclay Report, 1982, para 13.6.)

Taking this broader definition of community, think about which communities are important to you.

Although the community care legislation does not actually define 'community' (perhaps it assumes that everyone knows what it means) it can be gleaned from its content that locality, kinship, informal relationships and giving and receiving services all play their part.

The term 'care' is also surrounded by difficulties. It can be suggested that there are two main aspects of 'care'; the first refers to caring about people and the second refers to caring for them. It is quite possible to care about people; caring for them in the sense of attending to their needs is rather more personal and time consuming. The 'care' in 'community care' seems to refer to both. Where does all of this leave 'community care'?

Community care in its ideal form again has two threads: care *in* the community and care *by* the community. Care *in* the community stresses providing services to people in their own homes rather than in institutions. Where, for whatever reason, people cannot be cared for in their own homes, care should be provided in small homely settings. This thinking is reflected in the government's White Paper *Caring for People*, which states:

Community Care means providing the services and support which people who are affected by problems of ageing, mental illness, mental handicap or physical or sensory disability need to be able to live as independently as possible in their own houses or in 'homely' settings in the community. (Caring for People, para 1.1.)

This kind of care, in its ideal form, is not a cheap alternative to residential care. It is a means of providing people with a better quality of life, but in order to do so it needs to be well planned and adequately resourced.

Care *by* the community brings with it the implication that support will come from within the neighbourhoods or other communities in which people live through the networks which exist there. A great deal of care is just this, but a policy of community care exists to support such networks in order that they can continue to function and to be there when they either do not exist or fail to provide the necessary support. This again means that to function well community care has to be organised and well planned. If community care means leaving care to the community then the most vulnerable people will slip through the net because they do not possess support networks in the first place. Bulmer (1987) pointed out that in terms of informal care, people care for people they care *for*. Neighbourhood schemes therefore depend upon people providing care to the people informal carers do not care for and in this sense community care needs to be organised and planned within a strategy of community care.

Key factors which have influenced policy and provision

Present day community care policy and provision has evolved over many years. In order to understand the present it is very useful to see the growth of the idea from the 1960s onwards when the idea gathered momentum. Although cynically it is possible to see the community care movement as a way of saving money it is, at its best, not a cheap option. Griffiths (1988) whose report was commissioned by the government in the lead up to the National Health Service and Community Care Act 1990, did not see community

care as necessarily a money-saving exercise but as a way of spending resources in a more satisfactory way and of giving optimum quality of life by concentrating resources upon those most in need. It was not Griffiths, however, who drafted the resulting legislation.

Here I have chosen the key factors which paved the way to community care thinking.

Ideas about deinstitutionalisation

During the 1960s there were many well publicised reports and books which documented the worst features of institutionalisation and its effects upon people. The work of Goffman (1961) has already been mentioned in Chapter 1. He drew attention to what happened to many people who spent a long time in institutional care: depersonalisation and block treatment resulting in apathy, lack of initiative, inability to make personal plans, deterioration in personal habits, loss of contact with the outside world with a consequent loss of friends and possessions. Townsend (1962), in *The Last Refuge*, presented damning evidence of the dreadful conditions existing in many homes for elderly people. Maxwell Jones, at Dingleton Hospital in Melrose, successfully promoted a more community-based service for psychiatric patients, setting up multi-disciplinary teams and making domiciliary visits and family assessments the basis of acute psychiatric work.

Realisation of the inappropriateness of residential home or hospital care for some groups of people

In the childcare field, Bowlby (1965) emphasised the need for family relationships which had an effect upon keeping children within their own families whenever possible; this thinking also affected policies relating to children with learning difficulties whose care in long-stay hospitals was gradually replaced by a social model of care emphasising support to families and care in the community. In the field of elderly care a policy of a mixture of nursing home, residential care and community care has gradually replaced the policy of placing elderly people with dementia on long-stay hospital wards where they not only block beds for those requiring medical treatment but also do not always receive care appropriate to their needs.

Drugs

In the 1950s and 60s improvements in drugs, especially in the treatment of some psychiatric illnesses such as schizophrenia, meant that people who had previously found it almost impossible to survive outside a hospital setting could now do so. Their survival in the community still depends, however, upon the existence of good community support and careful monitoring of their drugs regime.

Demographic change

Changes in the structure of the population have led to changes in the way in which the future care of those in need is seen. This is particularly the case in terms of the elderly population which is increasing at an unprecedented rate in proportion to the rest of the population. It has been estimated that by the year 2020 one-third of the population will be of pensionable age (Griffiths, 1991). This has focused thinking upon the need to provide services within the parameters of the resources available. A policy of community care is the result and it remains to be seen

whether this does in fact combine the fulfilment of need with an economical alternative to residential or hospital care.

Ideas about normalisation

Such ideas have provided a further impetus to the formulation of a philosophy of community care. Many argue, however, that community care does not go far enough and that normalisation, with its emphasis upon integration and valued means to valued ends, extends thinking beyond community care to thinking about restructuring society itself.

The National Health Service and Community Care Act 1990

Thus a combination of philosophical, practical, population and financial arguments has led inexorably towards present day thinking, policy and practice in relation to community care. The actual embodiment of some of this thinking, combined with political flavouring, is contained in the National Health Service and Community Care Act 1990. Of course, such an act does not just happen. It was preceded by several government reports and other pieces of legislation. Among the most significant of these, in relation to community care, were the Audit Commission Report of December 1986, *Making a Reality of Community Care* and the Griffiths Report of March 1988, *Community Care: Agenda for Action*. The Audit Commission Report – a consultative document upon which many organisations were asked to comment – makes very interesting reading and summarises the state of affairs in the 1980s in relation to public expenditure on care, as well as making suggestions for the future direction of care. Griffiths, who had access to this report, made several recommendations in relation to community care, many though not all, of which were later incorporated into the White Paper, *Caring for People* which formed the basis for the community care part of the National Health Service and Community Care Act 1990.

Key objectives

Although the Act received Royal Assent in 1990, it was not 'fully' implemented until 1993. In fact, truly full implementation is unlikely in the face of cuts in resources. The key objectives of the legislation are set out in the White Paper as follows:

- to promote the development of domiciliary, day and respite services to enable people to live in their own homes wherever feasible and sensible

- to ensure that service providers make practical support for carers a high priority

- to make proper assessment of need and good care management the corner-stone of high quality care

- to promote the development of a flourishing independent section, alongside good quality public services

- to clarify the responsibilities of agencies and so make it easier to hold them to account for their performance

- to secure better value for taxpayers' money by introducing a new funding structure for social care

These objectives indicate some changes about thinking in relation to social care, for example there is a stated objective of promoting the independent sector. This is part of a policy of providing a mixed economy of care where local authorities are no longer the main providers of care but will be able to buy in services from private and voluntary agencies. The fact that support for carers is to receive a high priority recognises that carers are an invaluable resource, especially if their interests are attended to and support is given before crises are reached. The promotion of domiciliary, day care and respite services should enable more people to remain in their own homes for much longer and so reduce the demands upon the residential services which can focus upon those in greatest need of them.

The role of local authorities

One very important recommendation of Griffiths (1988), which was incorporated into the Act, was that overall financial responsibility for community care should rest with local authorities. This has meant that social services departments in England and Wales and social work departments in Scotland now hold the pursestrings for the financing of most community care, with some financial responsibilities switching to them from the Department of Social Security (DSS) and from health authorities and health boards. This is intended to make planning for community care much easier, since finance is now under one umbrella, and to correct some of the strange anomalies which had developed under the old system. An example of one of these was the responsibility for financing people assessed as needing help living in private and voluntary homes. The relative ease with which money could be obtained from the DSS for residential, including nursing home, care meant that many people ended up in such care, often private, when community care may have been more appropriate. Residential care was the expedient solution because the money could be obtained to pay for it. Now most of this money is allocated to local authorities to pay for whatever kind of care a person is assessed to need.

Local authorities have other responsibilities under the Act and these are discussed briefly before going on to look at some examples of the kinds of things which are happening in the field of care as the Act is implemented. Local authority social services and social work departments have responsibility for:

1) The planning of community care. Three-year plans should set out objectives and should be formulated in conjunction with health and other agencies.

2) Assessing individual needs of those who may need domiciliary and/or day care services or residential or nursing home care. The emphasis is upon needs-led assessment rather than service-led assessment. Service-led assessments concentrate upon assessing someone for a specific service such as residential care or a home help, whereas needs-led assessments spell out needs for which appropriate services then have to be found. Although in theory this sounds a good idea, it can raise hopes of provision which cannot in the end be fulfilled. Many care workers with whom I have discussed this feel that an explanation should be given at the outset of a needs-led assessment of the limitations of resources which may

mean that the resulting package of care is not the ideal.

3) Working out packages of care resulting from assessments and ensuring that services are provided. Provision can be either by their own or other agency services.

4) Arranging nursing accommodation.

5) Setting up arm's-length inspection units to monitor the quality of services provided, thus ensuring quality of care.

6) Establishing and operating a complaints procedure.

7) Funding and encouragement of a mixed economy of care already discussed above.

Examples of community care

There follows a brief description of several projects to give some idea of the variety of things which fall within the community care arena.

A core and cluster project

Recently I visited a community care scheme called The P Core and Cluster Project and, although it was in the early stages of development, I was very impressed with the way in which care is planned. The main aims of the project are:

• to provide accommodation with care on a 24-hour basis to vulnerable elderly people ... who would otherwise probably be admitted to a residential home

• to provide care on a 24-hour basis

• to enable residents to live as independently as possible within a normal homely environment

• to prevent major and traumatic changes to residents' accustomed lifestyle

Accommodation is provided in ordinary housing in the community, in four clusters of four flats, each flat housing two people and connected to a community alarm system. These clusters are all in the same locality of a large city and are supported from a central 'core' by support staff. Also at the core a 20-place day centre is planned. This scheme is run by a Scottish local authority social work department. At present five people are resident with a final capacity for 32. Figure 4.1 gives an idea of the structure of the project.

The project has been thought about very carefully and the following are seen as the core principles of practice:

1) **Equity** – to take positive action to allocate resources justly and fairly in accordance with need in an area, care group and on an individual basis.

2) **Normalisation** – to endorse the rights of individuals to live as valued and equal members of their own local communities within their own home or within a homely environment and to avoid stigma.

3) **Choice** – to take positive action to create choices in meeting needs in the community, including choices in residential and nursing home care.

4) **Quality** – to ensure the delivery of services of the highest possible quality and maximum flexibility in response to the needs and wishes of users and carers.

This scheme is part of a spectrum of community care, which includes some residential care but also aims to replace some of this care, and for this reason alone it would be exciting. It is made more so by the enthusiasm of the project manager and support staff who have spent many years working in residential settings and were dissatisfied with some aspects of them in their present form. They were dissatisfied with the way that compromises had to be made and dissatisfied with them as places for the care of many elderly people who did not have dementia. They saw a lot of people who came into residential care as giving up. In contrast, people coming out of long-term residential care into the core and cluster project (three at present) have been rejuvenated and have very quickly relearned the skills of independent living. The project is evolving and adapting to presenting circumstances. Although

```
Cluster 1                    Cluster 2
  0 0                          0 0
  0 0                          0 0




              Core
               +
        20 day care places




Cluster 3                    Cluster 4
  0 0                          0 0
  0 0                          0 0
```

Figure 4.1: The core and cluster project

originally planned for elderly people, one mother in her 70s with a son with learning disabilities in his 40s, both of whom have needs to be met in terms of the community care legislation, have been accommodated within the scheme. The mother commented that she used to be frightened about being separated from her son because of her inability to provide the amount of care he needs. Now she is frightened that she might wake up one day and find that this project is all a dream!

One area which has required very careful work is that of links with the local community, and this theme is taken up in Chapter 9.

From this account it is useful to examine how this scheme fulfils the aims of the National Health Service and Community Care Act 1990:

- it is within the locality in which service users have previously lived

- it is providing homely settings in the community

- care is flexible and is provided as and when needed

- assessment for the project is needs led

- the project should eventually be cost effective, providing as much care as people need but not the same care for everyone

Centres for independent living

Jane Campbell, in *Community Care*, 7–13 December 1995, discusses the ideal of centres for independent living (CILs) for people with disabilities. These are:

... community-based organisations providing a range of services for both disabled and non-disabled people. The important point about CILs is that they are controlled by disabled people themselves, who are responsible for defining policies and delivering services.

A day centre

The Ghandi Hall Day Centre in Manchester is described in Lynch and Perry (1992). Research conducted by a Dr Das revealed that there were many members of the Asian community living alone. He visited 216 families over a two-month period:

I was really shocked at the pathetic state they were living in. I found that some were very frail. Many had not been out of their council flats for more than a year because they have no car and they are too frail to go by bus.

Dr Das tried to get funding to expand an existing small day centre specifically for elderly Asian people but was told by the Director of Social Services that they were welcome to use existing day care provision. This, according to Dr Das, was not a solution:

But they can't go there. They don't understand English and it would be out of the frying pan into the fire. They would just sit there and nobody would talk to them. There are differences in diet, religion, culture – differences in everything.

In 1990 social services provided £800 for the day centre, which was cut to £700 in 1991. Joint funding by three local health authorities and the local authority eventually provided £12,000 each year to meet running expenses, and the rest is found from voluntary sources. The centre runs two days a week and most people attend for three to four hours. Activities include bingo, exercise classes, television and video, and Indian films are hired for service users to watch. There is a benefits advice session once a week and visits from local doctors and health visitors, with interpreters where necessary. There is also a temple at the day centre so that people can pray, and a monthly coach trip. Attendance at the centre has greatly improved the quality of life for service users. The centre is heavily dependent on voluntary help.

This centre fulfils many needs under community care provision:

- it is part of a mixed economy of care in that provision is funded from several sources and the service is provided by a voluntary organisation

- it is a day care centre and plays a part in enabling people to continue to live in their own homes

- it raises the quality of life for service users and is needs led in its provision

- it is run in the community, for the community, by the community

A resource centre

Resource centres have recently become a more prevalent feature of community care provision. I visited the T Resource Centre with Sandra and her mother during their search for a place which Sandra would like to attend after completion of her present course at a further education college. Sandra has learning difficulties and is not ready to move to employment or to independent living but needs challenge,

interest and help to fulfil her potential. She travels independently and is able to cope with her own physical needs. Here is what we found at the resource centre:

- a welcoming environment and a philosophy of maximising individual potential

- an open door policy with a snack bar run by service users and open to the public

- a dining area for lunches, also open to the public

- a hydrotherapy pool not only for centre attenders but also for others who need this service – for example John from a local hostel, who is confined to a wheelchair because of cerebral palsy and has little ability to control his body movements

- a fully equipped flat to give practice in independent living and assist in developing skills which can be used in the real world

- a darkroom and video equipment to assist in the development of video and photography skills

- a quiet room, a room in which discussions can be held and an activities and art/craft room

The programme at the centre is devised afresh every year in discussion with service users. One of the advantages of the centre is that it is a completely new venture and has given scope for departure from traditional concepts of care towards a philosophy based on normalisation and the promotion of independence. Funding is predominantly from the local authority but additional funding for specific activities, equipment and outings is gained from other sources. Increasingly, funding concerns are not straightforward, with money gained from several places for any additions to basic service provision.

This centre is responding to community care in the following ways:

• it is a needs-led service

• it is a day centre for people who are living predominantly in their own homes or in small homely settings

• it is building up links with the community, seeing itself as a service in the community, for the community and, to a certain extent, by the community

Community care has not in practice brought all of the benefits which had been hoped for with the new dawn of the legislation. Resource shortages have played an important part in this; so have public attitudes. Diana Rose (1996), a service user and social researcher, takes up this point in discussing people with mental health problems:

From the point of view of many people with mental health problems, community care is a failure. No matter how good at coping users are, no matter how dedicated professionals may be, community care will never work until the community itself changes. As we look towards the next millennium, the task is to educate the community so users are treated with the dignity and respect they deserve. (Rose, 1996.)

Although there is both a good and a not-so-good side to the result of a community care policy, the 1990 Act does seem to have forever changed the way in which care is thought about, and many agencies have grasped the challenge to provide innovative and fulfilling solutions to sharing planning and implementation with service users.

Exercise 2

Research the provision of community care in your area for one service user group. Write in some detail about four community care resources saying what they provide and for whom, how to get in touch with the service and your evaluation of it in terms of fulfilling need and optimising quality of life.

Suggestions for further reading

• Lynch, B. and Perry, R. (1992) *Experiences of Community Care*. Harlow: Longman.

A book which is full of examples of community care projects, how they started, how they are run and how successful they are.

• Meredith, B. (1993) *The Community Care Handbook*. London: ACE books (a publication of Age Concern).

A clear and comprehensive book which moves from looking at the meaning of community care to an explanation of the legislation; it contains many useful case examples.

5 Communication, relationships and counselling

A good communicator . . . should be trustworthy, reliable and honest and most especially, a good listener.

WHEAL, 1994.

No matter what the theoretical model by which one human being attempts to be of help to another, the most potent and dynamic power for influence lies in the relationship.

PERLMAN, 1970.

What is communication?

It seems obvious to say that at the heart of social care is good communication, but what is really meant by this? A good starting point is to look at the concept of communication itself. 'Communication' has been variously defined. The *Oxford English Dictionary* tells us that communication is 'the imparting, conveying or exchange of ideas, knowledge etc. (whether by speech, writing or signs); interchange of speech', but of course communication is much more than this. Almost everything we are and do (including being silent) can communicate something to someone else. Here are some other definitions of communication:

Communication is a process of encoding, transmitting and decoding signals in order to exchange information and ideas between participants. (Owens, 1984.)

Communication occurs whenever persons attribute significance to message-related behaviour. (Mortenson in Civikly, 1981.)

Communication is sharing meaning. (Kelly, 1981.)

These definitions show that communication is not just about people talking to one another. It can take many forms as long as some sort of message is conveyed and received.

Verbal, non-verbal and symbolic communication

Communication can be verbal (words either spoken, written or signed) or non-verbal (every other form of communication including body language, eye contact and tone of voice). Lishman (1994) further distinguishes symbolic communication, also very important in any kind of care work, which refers to aspects of behaviour and presentation which convey messages to people about how much you care for and respect them. Messages conveyed through the way you dress, your punctuality and the kind of care environment you help to create are forms of symbolic communication. Some care environments clearly say to service users that they do not matter, by being institutionally ugly and unwelcoming. Others clearly show respect and care and enable people to feel that they are important and worthy as individuals.

The Oomph factor

Another form of communication, which could be included as a combination of verbal, non-verbal and symbolic communication but which I mention separately here, is what one of my colleagues, Ellen Lancaster, calls the Oomph factor. She states that social care values and principles, skills and practices in caring for people are not complete without this very important and essential ingredient. The Oomph factor or the human factor has many ingredients as shown in Figure 5.1 below:

1) **Enthusiasm** includes encouraging and having faith in others; energetic and inspired practice.

2) **Dedication** involves continual support and consistency.

3) **Vocation** emphasises a full commitment treating social care as 'not just a job'.

4) **Genuine interest** means being interested in *all* people, knowing people's likes, dislikes, frustrations, expectations; also truthfulness.

5) **Enjoyment** involves showing genuine pleasure in what you are doing; also sharing successes or even failures, however small or great.

6) **Positive self disposition** emphasises knowing yourself, being happy with yourself and striving to share happiness; also maintaining hope in yourself and in others.

Communication without oomph, however appropriate it may be, can convey less than total commitment. Most of this book is about communication and the chapter on the care environment, Chapter 8, is particularly about symbolic communication.

To illustrate the difference between

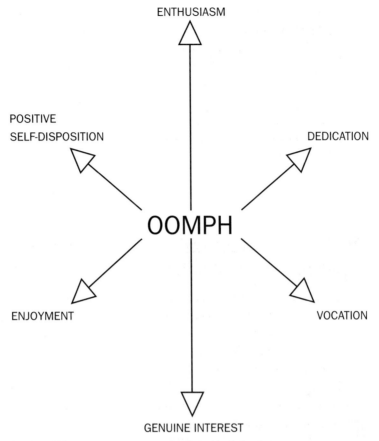

Figure 5.1: The Oomph factor – contributed by Ellen Lancaster

verbal and non-verbal communication take a simple question and answer:

- Q: How are you?

- A: I feel fine.

The verbal answer is easy to interpret. This person is fine ... or is she? If the answer is delivered in an absolutely flat voice and the respondent looks perfectly miserable, the non-verbal communication indicates that she is not fine at all. Here the way in which the words are spoken, their tone, is part of non-verbal communication, only the words themselves being verbal communication.

Care needs to be taken in interpreting non-verbal messages which are subject to cultural variations in much the same way as language, though in this example the non-verbal message is fairly clear ... or is it?

When I asked a group of social care students to tell me what they saw as communication, here is what they said. I have placed their suggestions into the three categories of verbal, non-verbal and symbolic, though they were not divided in this way at the time:

1) **Verbal communication** – conversation, sign language, Braille and talking synthesiser.

47

2) **Verbal and non-verbal communication** – listening.

3) **Non-verbal communication** – body language, including facial expression and eye contact, touch, behaviour, crying, withdrawing, intonation, expression and aggression.

4) **Symbolic communication** – atmosphere, general demeanour, approachability, acceptance, enthusiasm and love.

Some of these suggestions could arguably fall into at least two categories and the dividing lines are far from clear; nor is this a comprehensive list. It is just there to enable you to appreciate the range of things which might be considered to be communication and to encourage you to think about this.

This is purposely only a very brief introduction to communication. It is a huge subject and has been very well dealt with elsewhere. For further reading Thomson *et al.* (1995), Portch (1995) and Lishman (1994) are recommended.

Now I proceed to good communication in social care. What is 'good' communication? Before going any further write down your own thoughts on this.

In a paper entitled 'The Art of Social care', Jim Davidson, the unit manager of a home for elderly people, wrote the following about communication which applies to work in any setting:

The good communicator is many things. Within the field of social care however I feel s/he is one who enriches the life of another . . . No matter the communication system we adopt, all true communication in the caring field depends first and foremost

upon the person to person . . . we depend upon every level and type of communication. Anything that helps, comforts, supports, encourages, values and informs an individual is important in terms of communication. In the process of communication I believe we must be able, first and foremost, to communicate with ourselves. I am not suggesting that we all start talking to ourselves. I am sure more of us do that than we care to admit! But how can we communicate with others if we are not at ease or comfortable with ourselves? If we cannot value ourselves, how can we value others? If we cannot address that which is within us, how can we address others? Communication is about exchange, dialogue, interaction, information and union. It can also be anger, frustration, rejection, denial, argument and so many other negatives. Our task, however, is the promotion, with fellow workers, with relatives, other professionals and in particular with clients of communication in a way which promotes the dignity, the value, the importance of the other.

Examples of good communication

The following accounts are all about communication, among other things, and I hope that through demonstration a little of the essence of the excitement I felt at seeing good communication in practice will emerge.

Ben

Ben is a young man in his early 20s who is deaf, partially sighted and who has a degree of learning disability. He has no speech, though he can make signs and uses British Sign Language (BSL) as a form of communication. He lives in a residential unit run by a voluntary organisation. This unit is in a big, old house in a street of big, old houses and does not stand out, nor is attention drawn to it by signs outside.

Ben's keyworker has been very concerned to improve his quality of life and has, through communicating in every way possible (signing, touch, giving encouragement, time, company, sharing meals and activities), built up a trusting and beneficial relationship with Ben. One thing which it has been difficult to communicate to Ben has been any kind of continuity or structure to life. In order to enable Ben to participate fully in his own timetable of activities, and to empower him to exercise a degree of control over and choice about daily living, his keyworker suggested the idea of a day planner which they could work on together. This would enable Ben to shape his plans for each day and subsequently have some idea of what to expect from it. Since he only possesses a short memory span he can go to his planner to remind him about what he is doing next or at any particular time during the day.

What has emerged after a long, slow process of working together is an absolutely enormous, colourful day planner which is a magnetic board on the wall of Ben's room. There are symbols with words next to them for Ben to put on the planner to show all the things which he might do in a day, ranging from taking a shower or going to the day centre, to a trip to McDonald's. If something crops up which Ben has not done before, a new sign is made and introduced just before the activity.

A good deal of communication has already taken place: communication used in forming a relationship, communication to establish what Ben likes doing and the creation of a tool which communicates to Ben his plans for the day. But the tool is also being used as a further tool to enhance Ben's communication skills. He can say what he is going to be doing by indicating it on his day planner. The symbols for different activities are accompanied by words. Gradually, the symbols are becoming smaller and the words are becoming bigger so that eventually Ben will be able to recognise an activity by the word for it rather than a symbol.

Although this is a day planner the concept of further planning has been introduced. Ben is now able to anticipate up to a week in advance very confidently. He also participated in making his planner and helped to paint it when it was in its final stages. This communicated to Ben his worth as an individual and has also ensured that he has a respect for the end product of all this communication. Ben has destroyed many things in his time but has not ever tried to damage *his* planner. Its creation was built upon communication and relationship and has further enhanced both of these.

Tyn-y-Pwll

Another example which says a lot about good communication is Edward Donohue's (1985) inspiring account of life at Tyn-y-Pwll, a short-term residential project for young people aged 13–17 years', set in the hills of North Wales. The whole success of the project centred around communication, relationships, the promotion of equality and the fact that Tyn-y-Pwll quickly came to be seen as 'home' and not as an institution by those who came to stay. As Donohue states, Tyn-y-Pwll:

. . . was not just a short stay residential establishment or an intermediate treatment centre, it was a home where young people, staff and children, lived together and enjoyed life, albeit for a brief spell.

Communication at group meetings was especially important and rested upon the right of everyone to an equal say and the breaking down of the power relationships which often exist in residential settings. Donohue sees hierarchies as detrimental to communication, distorting communication between the 'top' and the 'bottom'. Tyn-y-Pwll had no hierarchies (which even some young people found hard to deal with at first) and this opened the doors to communication on a equal footing. Staff were prepared to listen to whatever young people had to say to them; not only to listen, but also to respond without loss of temper and with respect for the importance and relevance of what was said:

This question of two-way communication was very important at Tyn-y-Pwll and it was always the policy of the staff to find time to listen as well as to talk.

The programme at Tyn-y-Pwll was varied, full and fun and had among its objectives raising self esteem, increasing the ability of young people to cope in society and providing time out to reassess the present and future. Activities included canoeing, camping, fell walking, art and craftwork, drama and, of prime importance, group discussions. In order to give a flavour for the kinds of discussions which took place at Tyn-y-Pwll I have taken an example from one of the group meetings.

Joan, one of the group members, had spent some time in Holloway prison. The group members were very interested in this

and it got them talking about institutions in general. Joan firmly believed that Holloway had been no help to her at all and many of the girls in the group on that occasion shared similar views, not just about punitive institutions but about other institutions such as hospitals where they had often felt patronised and looked down on, and schools where they had often been excluded by teachers for lack of co-operation. From the way in which they talked about these institutional experiences it was evident that Tyn-y-Pwll was not included among them. The groups, over which care was taken to enable participants to feel safe, were not only forums in which to express views but also to face consequences of behaviour in a supportive setting.

Donohue summarises his thoughts on communication at Tyn-y-Pwll in the following way:

Good communication was considered to be essential. The young people were always listened to and the staff always tried to say what they meant and to mean what they said. They looked for non-verbal communications and tried to empathise, difficult though that was in some instances.

The Spanish brothers

One final example of good communication was given to me by a student working in a local authority home for elderly people. Two Spanish brothers, who spoke very little English, were admitted for a period of assessment and respite care. Initially, there was some resentment among some staff members about how difficult it was to communicate with these two very charming gentlemen. There seemed to be an attitude that 'if they can't speak English to us then we certainly aren't going to speak Spanish to them' ... not that anyone could.

The student then obtained a Spanish phrase book and tried out a few easy sentences. This was a source of amusement to the Spaniards but they were also highly delighted that someone had made the effort to communicate with them. Their whole demeanour changed, and from being rather depressed and quiet they became more cheerful and vocal. It did not actually take a great deal of effort to ask a few simple questions and, although the replies presented a certain amount of difficulty, the fact that some form of communication was taking place opened the door to the use of gestures, signs, touch and other forms of communication.

The example set by the student was then followed by other members of staff. Efforts were subsequently made to link the men with members of the Spanish community and to use a translator for discussions about future care. But it was the initial breaking down of the barrier posed by resentment, prejudice and ignorance which was perhaps the most important one in building the communication bridge.

Important points about good communication

The points which emerge about good communication from these accounts are as follows:

1) Good communication does not just happen. It needs to be thought about and optimised for each individual client.

2) All forms of communication are important: verbal, non-verbal and symbolic, and it is the combination of messages which people give and receive which need interpretation and thought.

3) Listening is at least as important as talking.

4) Enhancing the ability of the service user to communicate is a way of empowering the service user and increasing choice.

5) Hierarchies often present barriers to open and equal communication.

6) Social care workers who work with people who rely predominantly on sign language work best when they know that language and the different meanings which service users attach to signs.

7) Self knowledge and awareness of our own communication patterns enhance the ability to communicate with others.

8) Setting an example of good communication encourages others to do the same.

9) Working with people from different cultures and/or with a different language from the worker may be a challenge but should never be seen as a barrier.

10) Time for communication is vital. Care workers may not be able to set aside large quantities of the working day just for communication but they can show an openness to communication and should try never to be too busy to

listen. If everything which the service user wishes to say cannot be said at the time, a particular time for communication e.g. during a planned activity can, if possible, be set aside later on.

Relationships

Already, without specifically writing about relationships, a great deal has been said about their importance. For instance:

- the most effective communication takes place within a relationship of trust and respect

- sharing an activity like building a day planner can enhance the relationship between worker and service user

- the application of a model of planned care is unlikely to be effective unless it operates within the framework of a relationship

- relationships are very important

- relationships need work and do not just happen, any more than good communication just happens.

This is a beginning. What I would now like to examine is what constitutes the most helpful kind of caring relationship. What does a relationship need in order to maximise the service user's quality of life? This is the point at which writing about communication and writing about counselling meet, and a lot of what follows is fundamental to counselling as well as to any kind of communication and caring.

Demonstrating empathy

Empathy has already been introduced in Chapter 1, and I will expand a little upon what was said there. Some other expressions help to give a feel for its meaning. Through empathy the care worker is trying to help people by getting inside their skins and seeing the world through their eyes. This empathy needs the worker to listen to what the service user is saying and to be aware of non-verbal communication, then to respond in such a way as to demonstrate that what has been heard and observed is done from the user's point of view, not the worker's. The care worker also needs to ensure that the response has been received, for instance by asking a tentative, confirmatory question. All of this needs to take place in a safe and non-threatening way so that the service user is sufficiently at ease to express him or herself.

To give an example: if someone says to you 'I feel really unhappy about being here', a response which shows empathy would be to say 'Yes, I can see you're not feeling very happy here. Would you like to tell me a bit about what is making you unhappy?' Here the worker has picked up on the unhappiness and shows this by giving the user the opportunity to expand on what has been said. The service user's response will demonstrate whether or not he or she feels understood. If the worker had said something like 'Don't be silly. This is a lovely place. I'm sure you'll feel better in a week or two' the opportunity for discussion would have been lost and so would the makings of a meaningful helping relationship.

Often it is not possible to take up all of the things which service users bring up and the dismissive, 'everything will be all right', kind of answer is the easiest way out. But

Exercise 2

Invent replies to the following comments, first in a way which shows empathy and second in a way which does not:

- I'm worried about my daughter. I haven't heard from her for three weeks

- That worker, Mr Jones, keeps making suggestive comments to me and I don't like it

- I miss my husband. He died ten years ago but it seems just like yesterday

even just in passing the worker can show that he or she has heard and is trying to understand, while giving some indication that the matter will be taken up again when there is a bit more time.

Being genuine

This sounds obvious. People soon see through someone who is not genuine, who says one thing and then behaves in a way which completely contradicts this. Being genuine is about being yourself and about not pretending to be something or somebody else, not pretending to have skills you do not have, not pretending to care when you do not. It takes commitment to be genuine and a willingness to be honest when you do not know all the answers or what to do. Carl Rogers (1991), a major exponent of the person-centred approach in counselling, refers to this as *congruence*, the ability to be a real, genuine person, a person who does not need to pretend to be an expert or to feel superior in any way.

For example, Jenny, a social care worker in a home for elderly people, comes to

work in the morning and usually smiles at everyone and says a cheerful good morning, asks people how they are feeling and waits to hear their replies, and is upset with everyone else when a service user dies or becomes ill. She admits that there are parts of the job she would rather not do – cleaning up vomit is one task which gives her some difficulty – but she says that she tries to put herself in the other person's shoes in this situation and imagines that it cannot have been very pleasant to have been sick or to feel that someone else has to clear it up. Jenny shows many facets of the genuine care worker:

- what she says is consistent with what she does i.e. her non-verbal and verbal communication are in tune

- she behaves consistently so that people feel that they can rely on her

- she is confident in herself and is willing to acknowledge that there are some things she does not like doing

- she does not pretend and does not need to

- she is not defensive but is open and honest and if she is upset she has enough confidence to show this without being excessively demonstrative

- she is generally spontaneous and when she smiles she means it.

Showing warmth

Another thing which Jenny feels and shows is real warmth. This is not a dependent warmth but is part of her general approach to people shown through what Rogers (1991) calls *unconditional positive regard.* Here the worth of the person is unquestioned and the person is accepted without any conditions attached. Warmth is conveyed mainly through non-verbal communication and is rather difficult to describe in words.

How do you know when someone is showing warmth towards you? One way of showing warmth is through facial expression; smiling is very reassuring to most people. Empathy, being genuine and being attentive all convey warmth. Touch also is a way of showing warmth, though it is necessary to judge whether it is appropriate, whether people are comfortable with it and whether you, the worker are comfortable with using it. For some people who have been abused, touch may have bad memories associated with it, though it may still be used once difficulties have been talked through. Sometimes touch has sexual overtones which need to be resolved before it can become a useful way of conveying warmth.

For example, a social care worker in a home for elderly people felt that touch was misinterpreted by one elderly man who saw it as sexually suggestive. The service user had a mild form of dementia but the issue was discussed with him and the worker explained her difficulty in approaching him. He was able to comprehend in theory that his response had been inappropriate but unfortunately continued in practice to misunderstand any kind of physical contact. The worker in the end changed her normal practice in relation to this one person and avoided, for the time being, giving reassurance through touch.

For some people conveying warmth through touch is absolutely vital. Bob, who is both deaf and blind, would be unable to receive the worker's warmth in

any other way. It is also a very natural way of conveying warmth to children, especially those who do not have their own parents to do this. Snuggling up to read or tell stories or watch television and hugs at bedtime are important ways of conveying warmth. However, a word of caution; all of this has to be seen to be fairly distributed. Children who have a good deal of contact with their own parents and whom you may see as relatively stable can suddenly become exceedingly deprived when they consider that they are not getting their fair share of love. Getting it right is not entirely spontaneous.

Being responsive

Of course empathy, being genuine and showing warmth are all ways of being responsive. Under this heading all of the other aspects of the relationship which seem to be important are discussed. Listening, active listening, that is hearing not just what is being said but tuning in to the tone of voice, what is left unsaid and any areas which cause discomfort, is a component of communication and the relationship which is worth re-emphasising here. There is a need to check out with the person that what is being heard is what you are meant to hear. This can be done by summarising to the person what he or she has said (this takes practice) and tentatively asking if this accurate. For example, if someone spends a long time telling you about problems he or she is having with the person with whom he or she shares a room, you might want to summarise in the following way: 'You're saying that there are a lot of things you don't like about sharing a room with Mrs Smith. Am I right?' This gives the person the opportunity either to agree and continue or to say that that was not what was meant at all and to present the account in a different way.

Responsiveness is also about being culturally sensitive. Dervla Murphy (1987) explains how she became sensitive to the cultural chasms which divide people of different cultural groups in Bradford and Birmingham and how this affects their communication and perception of society. If some groups are constantly given negative messages – you're no good, you're not welcome, you're stupid – and if they are discriminated against in almost every aspect of life, then attitudes of rebellion or hopelessness or protection through isolation or ignoring what is happening become comprehensible. Knowledge of different cultural practices is an asset. But it is vital that practice rests upon a firm value base and that the social carer is sensitive to the possible implications of culture for behaviour. Dervla Murphy's example is interesting because as a travel writer she was not out to make any particular point about communication, racism or anti-discriminatory practice, yet she does make points about all of these with immense empathy and force.

The importance of encouragement and approval are often underestimated. Although social carers think that it is often enough to convey approval non-verbally through a smile or another gesture it is very helpful if this can also be verbalised. A statement like 'I think you're doing really well', or 'I love the painting you did today' can enable people to feel good about themselves. This also reinforces this behaviour and may lead to positive change and a rise in self esteem.

Counselling

Counselling is not something separate from communication and relationships. Both are a prerequisite to its application. Counselling is surrounded by all sorts of misconceptions. It is often viewed as though it is something sacred which ordinary mortals cannot do, i.e. you cannot counsel unless you have attended many counselling courses, had hundreds of hours of supervised experience and understand all of the psychological theories known to man. Herein lies some truth and a lot of myth. It is certainly the case that reading this chapter will *not* make you a competent counsellor. But it is also the case that counselling theorists have provided a lot of useful material about communicating with people and some models for working with people which can be useful to care workers in their practice. Certainly, if you wish to become a qualified and competent counsellor you should take a counselling course, or even two or three. But in the absence of this privilege it is useful to look at what counselling can teach us and how it can help in day to day work with people. I regard this as an introduction to counselling and hope that those who see it as worthwhile will follow it up.

(The remainder of this chapter was contributed by Carol Sallows, a counsellor/social worker with The Women's Counselling and Resource Service, Glasgow City Council Department of Social Work.)

What is counselling?

The British Association for Counselling defines counselling as:

> *. . . when a person occupying regularly or temporarily the role of counsellor, offers and*

agrees explicitly to give time, attention and respect to another person, or persons, who will temporarily be in the client role.
(British Association of Counselling, 1985.)

However, this is just one definition of a word which can have several different meanings. It can also be defined as 'a way of helping people to find and use their own resources for coping with difficult situations', or as 'a way of helping somebody learn to live (a bit) more effectively.' Individual counsellors will have their own particular approach based on theories such as the behavioural, psychodynamic, person-centred, cognitive-behavioural, feminist and the three stage model. The well known person-centred model (Rogers, 1991) and the three stage skills model (Egan, 1986) will be described later in this chapter.

One of the most important aims of counselling is to help people become more aware of their own personal resources so that they can be more confident about making decisions in their lives. Counselling could therefore be described as a process of empowerment, in which people are given the opportunity to take greater control over their own lives. Helping them make their own choices rather than giving them advice or telling them what to do is the basic characteristic of counselling. In order to make choices people need information. This could be obtained during a one-off visit to an information or advice centre or by approaching an appropriate service of the social work, social services, health service or voluntary sectors.

Alternatively, counselling may take place on a regular basis for a longer period of time. The issue may be in relation to

resolving a conflict, perhaps between partners, or helping someone explore their feelings as a result of sexual abuse. It may also take the form of allowing a person to grieve, following the loss of a significant individual in his or her life. The aims of counselling therefore might involve assisting the person to develop and grow, to raise his or her awareness or offer support. All of the values and principles implicit in good social care practice are essential to counselling and the practice of counselling skills. A warm and trusting relationship must exist for individuals to feel safe enough to disclose and explore their personal thoughts and feelings.

Skills of counselling

Counselling skills are relevant to a wide range of social care settings, from the informal chat over a cup of coffee with a service user – perhaps a tenant in a group care setting – to the more formal meeting which might take place on a regular basis with, for example, a young person in a children's home. These meetings would involve the practice of the range of counselling skills.

Such skills are not particularly distinguishable from social, communication and interpersonal skills. Listening, active listening, paraphrasing, using open questions and reflective responding are skills used in counselling. These can be improved with practice and self reflection. Are you able to let a person finish talking without reacting? Are you able to listen without interrupting?

LISTENING
Listening can be difficult as we sometimes feel the need to respond prematurely to resolve the person's difficulty or to move

the interview on for a variety of reasons. There may also be occasions when we feel tired, hungry, harassed or have other personal matters on our mind, and this too will hinder our ability to listen effectively. One of the most common barriers to accurately receiving a person's messages is the worker's or helper's own values. It is therefore essential that as care workers we regularly inspect and review our own set of values.

ACTIVE LISTENING

Active listening involves not only passive hearing but also responding to what has been said, and acting on it. This can assist the person to move the interview forward. Active listening includes skills of paraphrasing, reflective responding, summarising, focusing and using open questions.

PARAPHRASING

Paraphrasing is a way of expressing what the person feels by saying it back to them in your own words.

REFLECTIVE RESPONDING

Reflective responding is being able accurately to reflect the content of what has been said as well as the person's feelings, and not what you *think* has been said or how you might have interpreted the person's words. It is important that the helper notes his or her tone of voice and body language.

SUMMARISING

Summarising can mean different things at different stages of counselling. The summarising that goes on in the first stage is a fairly passive process of showing and checking with the person that you understand the problem. Summarising at a later stage involves keeping all the key strands of the concern in mind.

Exercise 3

This exercise is to be done with a partner and, if possible, also with an observer who can comment upon it afterwards. The exercise should last no longer than three minutes.

Ask your partner to talk about a problem, real or imagined, for about three minutes in total. Listen actively and at the end of each minute, or thereabouts, paraphrase what you understand to have been 'said', both verbally and non-verbally i.e. feed back what has been said and otherwise communicated to you, in your own words.

At the end of three minutes summarise what you have understood your partner to be saying and ask if that is accurate. Ask your partner how he or she feels about you as the counsellor. Did he or she feel understood? Note how long three minutes seems and how difficult it is to restrict yourself to paraphrasing and summarising. Did you want to present a 'solution' to the problem? If an observer was present ask for feedback on how successful you were. Practise this several times so that you feel confident in active listening, paraphrasing and summarising.

OPEN QUESTIONS

Open questioning does not come easily and to do it involves thinking ahead. For example, open questions as in 'how are you feeling today?' give more scope for the person to respond in his or her own way rather than the closed question of 'are you feeling better today?', which is more likely to elicit a 'yes' or 'no' response. Closed questions discourage the person from talking and create silences, which can result in the helper asking yet more questions.

Exercise 4

Turn the following closed questions, which invite a 'yes' or 'no' answer, into open questions:

1) Do you like coming here?

2) Are you feeling well today?

3) You do like Bingo, don't you?

Now make a list of open questions which you might use with service users to encourage them to talk about their feelings and concerns.

In using the above skills, care workers should be able to assist service users to feel that their circumstances are being accepted and understood.

On the spot counselling

Social care settings present many opportunities for counselling both individuals and groups within the everyday life of the establishment. There are natural opportunities, often rather short in time, which lend themselves to significant counselling of service users by workers. It does, however, take the ability of the worker to recognise these opportunities, sometimes to create them, and use them without letting them pass by. This is not an easy task since if emotive material is brought up when you are very busy, the ability to deal with it has to be balanced against the needs of other service users and other tasks which must be performed. Sometimes full discussion has to be delayed but what is being said should not be ignored.

On the spot counselling can prevent many later problems. For example, care workers can be expected to provide immediate counselling support for service users who are showing distress by behaving in an unusual, difficult or disruptive manner, as in an elderly person arriving distressed at a day centre. Another example of on the spot counselling might involve responding to the casually expressed concerns of a service user during a meal about a recent or forthcoming event. The role of the carer would be to help reduce the level of stress.

Exercise 5

Give counselling support to someone who is distressed e.g. someone who is very upset upon arrival at a day centre, or someone who has accidentally dropped something and is very agitated as a result of this.

Counselling models

PERSON-CENTRED

Carl Rogers (1991) developed the idea of 'client-centred', 'non- directive', or perhaps more commonly known 'person-centred' counselling. The idea behind this theory is that counselling is a way of being with people and not something you would do to people. Rogers refers to the 'core conditions of counselling' which are necessary for an effective counselling relationship, together with some of the above mentioned skills. The core conditions may be regarded as personal qualities or dispositions, which can be learned through reflection and through practice with others.

The core conditions are empathy, unconditional positive regard (warmth, acceptance and respect) and congruence (genuineness), all of which have been discussed in this chapter in the section about relationships. It was Rogers' sincere belief that individuals have the ability to control their own lives and the innate potential to be self directing, and that it is the task of the counsellor, through empathy, congruence and unconditional positive regard to enable people to reach this potential. A counsellor cannot just pay lip service to this but must have incorporated it into his or her personality, otherwise he or she cannot become a person-centred counsellor. The counsellor is not directive or controlling in any way, and allows people to move at their own pace and make their own choices. This is not, however, a passive approach since the counsellor is fully attentive to what the person is communicating and shows understanding and acceptance. Another of Rogers' beliefs was in the 'actualising tendency' – the inclination of people to move towards fulfilment if only they can be given the opportunity. For some people who have little faith in themselves, low self esteem can prevent them from self-actualising. Rogers felt that although previous experience might have failed them, self belief could be an outcome of the counselling process.

THREE STAGE SKILLS MODEL

Gerard Egan's three stage skills model of helping provides a framework for assisting people to deal with their difficulties. Egan's model is based on the premise that people take ultimate responsibility for seeking solutions to their difficulties. If the person is helped to develop a sense of personal responsibility and self reliance he or she is more likely to benefit in the long term.

- **Stage 1** the first stage, which is the exploration stage, involves the counsellor helping the person to explore the area of concern so that it becomes clear. People are known to approach counselling with the realisation that they have a problem while often being unaware of exactly how it has come about or how to deal with it. The task therefore for the counsellor during this phase of the work is to understand the person. Through empathic, accepting responses, a relationship of trust should develop between the counsellor and the person which allows the process of exploration to take place. At the end of this stage a clear picture of the problem or concern should begin to emerge. Appropriate helping skills at this stage would include active listening, communicating empathy, demonstrating acceptance, being genuine, paraphrasing, reflecting, summarising and using open questions. Demonstration of the above skills should help the person to feel comfortable so that he or she can move forward. Noticing people's body language will help the counsellor to be more in tune with them and their feelings. It is also important that the counsellor be aware of his or her own body language.

- **Stage 2** in the second stage, developing new understanding, the counsellor's role is to help the person see him or herself from new perspectives and to develop a deeper understanding. This allows the person to decide what might be done about the area of concern, leading eventually to specific goals or objectives being set. By the end of this stage, the problem should be seen by the person in new ways and stated in different terms.

People often have their own interpretation and explanation for difficulty which may stem from a lack of self esteem. They may blame themselves for their difficulties and the counsellor can help them examine this in a new light. Seeing things from a fresh angle can often help to replace the lethargy and depression, which arises from feelings of helplessness, with a new energy and willingness to take action. At this stage, all of the skills of Stage 1 remain relevant, but there is a shift in emphasis toward challenging the person so that he or she can move forward. These skills are sometimes known as challenging skills and include summarising, appropriate sharing about self, offering information, immediacy (what is happening in the here and now between counsellor and person) and goal setting.

Summarising involves the counsellor feeding back to the person the key issues that have taken place so far within the counselling session. Self disclosure is the process of communicating thoughts and feelings about one's attitudes. It means knowing at what point and to what extent the counsellor should offer information about him or herself within the counselling session. Positive self disclosure can be effective in initiating and maintaining warm, genuine and empathic relationships and can be communicated by facial expressions, gaze, gestures, body language and tone of voice. In this stage it is important to risk hunches, pick out themes, put two and two together, make the implicit explicit, and identify the meaning behind the words. It is essential at this stage to provide the correct balance between challenge and support for the person, and any form of challenge should be done in a way which indicates the counsellor's sense of caring for the person.

- **Stage 3** in the third stage, the counsellor's role is to help the person to translate the goals previously identified into specific action plans. This is done by examining different ways of achieving the goals. In this process, the counsellor helps the person to identify personal resources and assets. At this stage, all the skills of Stage 2 remain relevant, as well as the skills of creative thinking, problem solving and decision making. By the end of this stage, the problem should have been managed. It is important however that the goals the person sets are realistic and within the person's control.

Exercise 6

In your work setting or placement pick up on casually stated worries, for example if someone expresses concern about an outing during a meal time. Try to find ways of reducing the stress through demonstrating empathy, warmth and unconditional positive regard. Write about this afterwards and also try to discuss your thoughts with a colleague, supervisor or tutor.

This exercise, and the other exercises in this section, do not even begin to cover all the skills of counselling, but do provide practice in skills which can be used to help service users to move forward in coping with problems in social care settings. These skills and all of the others associated with communication and counselling require a great deal of practice both in simulated and real situations. The best way to gain this practice is to take an organised counselling course where supervision can be provided by experienced counsellors. The importance of supervision is further emphasised in Chapters 8 and 11.

Suggestions for further reading

- Hough, M. (1994) *A Practical Approach to Counselling*. London: Pitman Publishing.

  This provides a good overview of many different approaches to counselling with interesting comment about the people who originated the theories.

- Inskipp, F. (1988) *Counselling Skills*. Cambridge: National Extension College.

  An introductory course in counselling with audiotapes and lots of exercises; can be used with groups or for self directed study and contains very good materials.

- Nelson-Jones, R. (1993) *Practical Counselling and Helping Skills*, 3rd edn. London: Cassell.

  A clearly written book which is widely used on counselling courses. There is also a separate training manual with 100 practical exercises.

6 Assessment and care planning

... we are endeavouring to help the client to feel: 'This is my assessment of aspects of my life which you are helping me with in order that I can have better services from you'...

Seed and Kaye, 1994.

One of the main aims of this chapter is to enable social care workers to understand and to participate fully in the assessment and care planning process. It also aims to encourage workers to maximise the sharing of this process with service users, for it is essentially their assessment. Assessment should not be *of* someone but *with* someone or a group of people.

What does assessment mean? Essentially it means an exploration of needs and opportunities as part of the process of care in order to enable the service user to reach a quality of life which is as good as it can be. A good assessment will also take into account the needs and opportunities of those in the immediate environment, such as family and other carers. Sometimes an assessment has to be a balancing act involving the needs of several people and may involve compromise, but essentially the focus is on the service user; the assessment is with that person and the aim in the end is to maximise quality of life.

Imagine that you are the manager at a review of someone who has very severe communication problems and has opted not to be present. She is represented by her keyworker who, when asked for her contribution to the assessment and care planning process says 'She's fine'. Can you be satisfied with that? It is hoped that this chapter will enable social care workers to make contributions to the assessment and care planning process which ask questions about whether care is as good as it can be, which analyse areas where choice may be offered and which indicate that there has been as much communication as possible and that maximum opportunity has been provided for the service user to express his or her views.

Needs-led and service-led approaches

As with everything else in social care the nature of the assessment and care planning process is changing. The National Health Service and Community Care Act 1990 laid emphasis upon needs-led assessment. This is having a profound impact upon thinking about assessment, even though the outcome may not always be that different from the outcome of an assessment made before the Act was implemented. In the past, people were often assessed for a particular service. For instance, a referral would be received by a social services or social work department to assess a service user for residential care or a home help. This has become known as a service-led assessment. The title of an article 'Assessment of Elderly People for Residential Care' (Miller and Grant, 1972) is an example of the former academic and practical acceptability of this approach. But who could write such an article now in the wake of the 1990 legislation and its more recent implementation in 1993? Now a referral would be for an assessment of a service user's needs. The service outcome may be the same as it would have been before, or it may be very different – what is certainly different is the approach. The post-1990 approach has become known as the needs-led approach and focuses upon a full examination of needs in the broadest sense: physical needs, intellectual needs, emotional needs, cultural and social needs and some psychologists see language as a separate, additional need. Only when this has been completed with the maximum involvement of the service user is a plan developed and action taken.

The 1990 legislation also laid emphasis upon care management and co-ordination. This is essentially about one person taking overall responsibility for the assessment even though many people may contribute to it. A care manager can be anyone with the ability to undertake the task and, as social care workers grow in competence and confidence and become better trained and better qualified, it becomes increasingly likely that they will co-ordinate assessments as well as participate in them.

Full and partial assessments

In many group care and community settings, assessment processes are already in place. Sometimes these processes are full needs-led assessments, but just as often they are partial assessments which only play a part in the total assessment picture. For example, many agencies working with people with learning difficulties complete an assessment with a name like 'Irabeena' or 'Copeland' which assesses competence in tasks of daily living. These assessments, consisting of long lists of tasks, broadened into component parts with columns to tick off competence, may prove useful in setting tasks to be achieved but should not be regarded as showing the total picture. They are only one tool, among a number of tools which will be examined later, which contribute towards a full assessment.

Other examples of partial assessments are those which aim to produce an optimum quality of life for a service user at present in a particular setting. For example, while Susan, aged eight, is in Elmtree Home, there will be an assessment resulting in a plan of how best she will live her days and weeks in the home. However, this is only part of a much larger assessment contributing to an overall plan of care in the long term, with a possible return home to her mother as the end result. Overall assessment and plan and partial assessment and plan will influence one another. Similarly, someone staying in a hospice for respite care will be assessed in terms of how daily life can best be spent while in the hospice, while the period of respite care is part of a long-term plan of care in which that person spends as much time at home as possible.

Both full and partial assessments are of

importance, and while not all social care workers may carry responsibility for care management they will be involved in assessments with a view to optimising the service user's quality of life while in their care. These partial assessments play a vital role in care management.

Assessment as part of a model of care

Assessment is one element in a model of care which includes assessment, care planning, implementation and evaluation. Figure 6.1 simplifies the process involved and illustrates the importance of a firm value and knowledge base at the root of good social care practice.

Principles – including those of choice, confidentiality, empowerment and rights – are as important in the assessment and care planning process as they are in any other aspect of care. Knowledge will include knowledge of human development, policies, services, the local environment and some sociological and psychological theory. Although this knowledge base does not form part of this book it can usefully be found elsewhere (see Thomson, 1995 and Haralambos, 1995). Skills too of communication, counselling and implementing care plans form part of the foundation of the caring model. The relationship built up between social care worker and service user also plays an invaluable part in the assessment process. An assessment which takes place within a tried, trusted and enduring relationship where there is positive communication among the participants is more likely to result in the sharing of information and an understanding by participants of how needs can be met to fulfil the best possible quality of life. Only with these

foundations can the process of assessing, planning, implementing and evaluating take place. The process is a circular one in that it should never be regarded as complete. Evaluation, which takes place through monitoring and review, may lead to changes in the assessment and resulting plan of care.

Important points about assessment

Before looking at tools of assessment it seems useful to summarise points about the assessment process. This list has resulted from discussions with social care workers and service users about their own experience of the assessment process:

1) Assessment should rest upon a firm value base, with respect for the dignity of every individual at the forefront. It should therefore incorporate choice, empowerment, risk taking, confidentiality, a non-judgemental approach and the practice of other social care principles.

2) Good communication is essential to good assessment. This involves active listening, empathy, honesty, open-mindedness and observation. The best assessments take place within a relationship of trust and respect.

3) Assessment is *with* and not *of* the service user.

4) Assessment should be on-going with a need for constant monitoring and reviewing. It is a continuing thing, not a static event.

5) Assessment is the basis for planning.

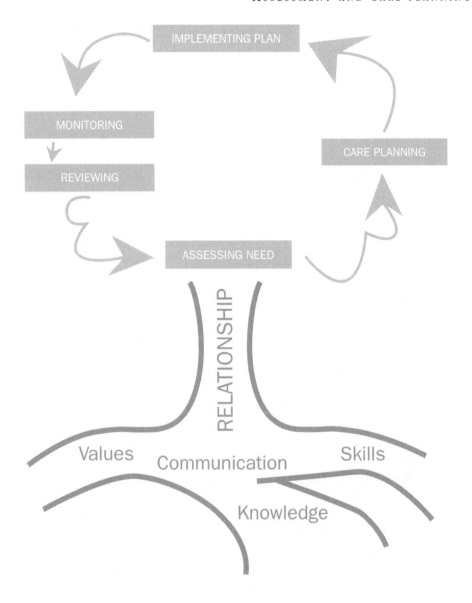

Figure 6.1: The tree of a model of care practice

6) Assessment aims to identify and understand need. It should be needs led and not service led.

7) Accuracy of factual information is essential. It is important to distinguish clearly between what is fact, and what is opinion, intuition or something else.

8) Information used in assessment should be as up to date as possible.

9) The social care worker should be very

65

careful not to label, stigmatise or make a scapegoat of a person in an assessment.

10) Assessments should be available and belong to the service user concerned. Whenever possible the assessment should be written using 'I' for the person's statement of needs.

Tools of assessment

Assessment is not a mechanical exercise and should be carried out in circumstances which create as little stress as possible. To this end it is useful for the social care worker to appreciate that there are various tools which can make the whole process not only relevant but also enjoyable. At one end of the assessment tool spectrum there is form filling and this does have its uses in providing needed factual information. There are, however, other equally useful tools. All of these tools will be examined below in terms of their merits and disadvantages.

Assessment forms

There is nothing intrinsically either good or bad about having forms available for assessment purposes. They may record information which is useful to the assessment process such as personal details, information about health, background history, family details and so on.

There may be different forms for different parts of the assessment process, for example one which has summary introductory information and one which summarises needs at the end. The important points to remember about forms are:

- they should not be allowed to control the assessment process

- they should ask only for the information required for assessment purposes

- they should as far as possible set out information about the service user as if he or she is writing, i.e. information about 'me'

- all information should be dated

- the source of information should be clearly shown.

I have purposely resisted the temptation to give examples of forms since there is a danger that they will be used for purposes for which they were not designed. Agencies should develop forms which serve their own purposes in the assessment of service users. These forms should be sufficiently flexible to allow for additional information which may be relevant. Areas covered should be broad and allow for flexibility in the way information is presented and what type of information is presented. The final assessment form could be a summary of needs, what Seed and Kaye (1994) have called a summary needs profile. This draws together information gained through the use of many tools of assessment.

Checklists

The advantages and pitfalls of forms apply also to checklists. They have their uses but can be restrictive especially if they come to be seen as *the* assessment. The examples of 'Irabeena' and 'Copeland' have already been given. Care workers working with service users with profound learning difficulties have often preferred to devise their own skills checklists since they have found that the standard ones are not relevant or useful to their own service user group.

Observation

Nobody wishes to feel like a goldfish in a bowl: looked at, analysed, reported on and, of course, fed at appropriate times. However, noticing the service user's behaviour, physical condition and personal circumstances can be of great benefit in assisting towards an optimum quality of life. If it is observed that a person appears uncomfortable when the television is switched on, when there is a lot of noise, when certain people are present, then these observations can be discussed. If they require action then this can be incorporated into the plan of care. Alternative activities, places to sit and different company can be arranged. If it is observed that George, for example, usually a talkative and lively man, is looking pale and lethargic and is not talking to anyone, he can be asked how he feels and help given or called in if this is thought to be appropriate. If he continues to act differently there may need to be changes to his plan of care.

Observation merely requires the social care worker to be observant and to discuss where possible any observations which may be of significance to the service user's quality of life. It should always be against a background of respect for the individual, his or her choice and privacy, and should not usually require any setting up of specific situations for observation which could be both obvious and threatening. However, it is recognised that sometimes the only practical way to see how a person copes in a particular situation is to set up something. For example, if George has not

cooked for himself for a long time and is considering returning to his own flat, it may be useful to see how he gets on in the kitchen and whether he can cope with cooking some of his own meals.

Asking questions

Asking questions about what people need and want is one of the quickest and most direct ways of gaining information which can be included in an assessment. If the questions are thought out carefully and relate to areas which are important in the person's life, the information gained can be extremely useful. Some information is perhaps best gained through asking questions, for example factual information about housing situation, services received as well as essential information about name, age and so on. Wheal (1994) lists areas about which children in care answer a set of questions: health, education, identity, family and social relationships, emotional and behavioural development and self care skills. Other information is gained just as well in one of the more informal methods detailed below and in a far less threatening way. Asking a lot of questions in a formal situation can seem very intimidating and may only elicit what the service user thinks you wish to hear . . . or perhaps only what you do not wish to hear – it depends on the individual. Questions may not, in fact, produce a very accurate picture of need and should, whenever possible, be supplemented by information gained through other means.

Diary of the social care worker

By keeping a diary for a set period of time in relation to a specific service user, the social care worker or workers can perhaps begin to see patterns of behaviour, causes and effects, issues which are of importance, social contacts, likes, dislikes and needs which may not have been previously evident. Writing things down is a very good way to clarify thinking and to begin to analyse what is important in any plans of care in the present and the future. Setting a time limit is useful because once something is known to have an end and a purpose it is more likely to be kept up and the aim achieved. Seed and Kaye (1994) suggest that a diary could be kept for 14 days, and this would seem to be long enough to record most activities and to be representative. One week would be too short and may represent an unusual week, and more than two weeks would place too much demand on the care worker.

Diary of the service user

For the same period of time during which the social care worker is keeping a diary it is also useful for the service user to keep one. This assumes the ability to do this and that the user does not mind the diary being used for assessment purposes. If the service user is not able to keep a diary it is often possible for another worker, relative or friend to help. Again, writing things in diary form, though it may seem to be a descriptive exercise of the 'what I did today' variety, may enable service users to pick out what is important to them, to see for instance that they feel better about some days or activities than others, to say things in writing which they may not mind the social care worker seeing but which they would not have the courage to say out loud. The diary may also serve the purpose of developing literacy skills in an enjoyable way.

Other diaries

Others may be involved in caring; for instance in shared care situations where a service user spends some time at home and some time with another family, family members and carers could keep diaries indicating areas of need both for the service user and family members.

Network analysis

Philip Seed (1990) has developed the use of networks both as a tool of assessment and as a means of implementing plans. The information for creating a picture of the service user's contacts and activities gained from all sources, including diaries, can be summarised in the form of a network diagram, which shows the network in existence and may indicate gaps in the network which the service user would like filled but is unable to fill without help. For example, there may be a significant person with whom no contact is shown in the network diagram. There may be many reasons for this but it may be a desirable outcome to remedy this situation. No-one may have realised the significance of that person, there may have been insufficient staff available to assist the service user to visit that person, or the person him or herself may not have realised that the service user wished to maintain contact. Ideas about networks are further developed in Chapter 7.

Personal history flowchart

This may not be useful with everyone but for some it may point out the degree of disruption which has taken place in their lives and indicate crises or transitions which have not been adequately dealt with. A fictionalised version of a flowchart, shown in Figure 6.2, is not far short of the true picture for many children in care.

A personal history flowchart of Susan, aged 13

Born 5 August 1982 (5 weeks' prematurely), the second child of John and Karen. There is an older sister, aged 2. Lives with parents and sister in a flat in an area of a large city which has a lot of problems.

↓

8 months: father leaves to live with girlfriend. Mother can't cope on her own and moves in with her parents.

↓

14 months: mother takes up own tenancy near her parents.

↓

18 months: father returns. Both parents drinking heavily. Susan and her sister have frequent stays with their grandparents.

↓

4 years: child abuse investigation; children found to be neglected and are taken to emergency foster parents in another part of the city.

↓

4 years, 6 months: Susan and her sister return home.

↓

5 years: child abuse investigation; physical abuse confirmed; children go to different foster parents; grandparents in poor health and unable to help.

↓

3 weeks later: foster parents find Susan's behaviour too disruptive and she is moved to local children's home.

↓

7 years: Susan returns home where the situation is found to be more stable. Contact with both parents has been maintained during her time in care.

↓

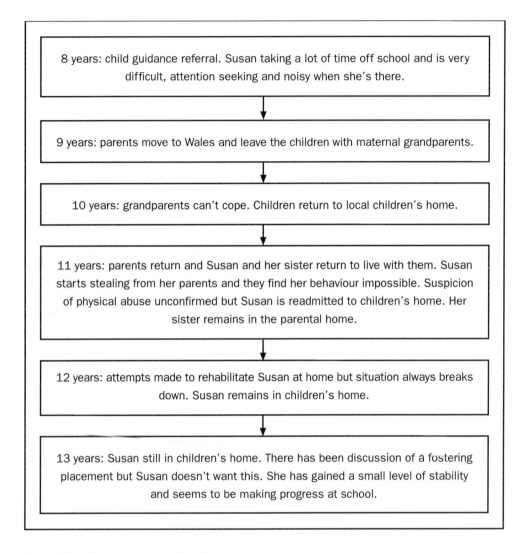

Figure 6.2: A personal history flowchart

Exercise 1

1) What are your observations about this flowchart?

2) How does this chart help in the assessment process?

Group discussions

Group discussions are often very useful in the assessment process and their part can be greatly underestimated. Tom Douglas (1978) has outlined the many advantages of working with people in groups rather than on a one to one basis. Some of these advantages apply also to the use of groups in the assessment process. Among the advantages are the following:

1) People can often clarify their own ideas, needs and wishes in discussion in a group setting in which they receive encouragement and stimulation from the presence and contributions of others.

2) People may feel more confident in expressing their ideas in a group with others than on their own with a worker.

3) The group plays a particularly important part when part of the assessment of need and provision of a service relates to the group as a whole. For example, the basic needs of food and shelter are often things catered for on a group basis even though they affect all individuals in the group. The best solution for everyone may only be arrived at through bringing the issues to the group as a whole. This does not replace the need also to discuss these things on a one to one basis.

The group discussion may not be the answer for everyone: some people may *never* say anything in front of a group, a group can be dominated by the views of one or two outspoken people and for some individuals it just is not a good source of information. The group discussion should never therefore be relied upon as the sole source if information.

Shared activities

Some of the best assessments take place when the aim is not assessment at all. A shared activity can be an important focal point in an assessment with or without its being set up for this purpose. Cooking, playing together, doing something the service user really likes to do, often encourages an openness and a relaxed atmosphere in which people feel at ease enough to talk about their wishes or needs and, where there is sufficient diversion in the activity concerned, to escape into it if the conversation becomes difficult or too emotionally charged.

CASE EXAMPLE – JOHN

John, a 13-year-old in a children's home, enjoyed baking with his keyworker. It was an opportunity for both of them to discuss what John hoped for from the future. He was able to tell his keyworker that he wanted to go back to live with his mother and stepfather but he knew that it would be difficult because of trouble in the past. It was the beginning of enabling John to look at his own behaviour and it was an opportunity both for worker and John to explore possible courses of action in the future. The discussion resulted in tasks which could be incorporated into John's care plan.

CASE EXAMPLE – MAY

Although a bath is not perhaps what you would call a shared activity, it can be a time of sharing. If the atmosphere is relaxed and a person is unable to bath without assistance the bath can be the opportunity for conversation about issues which may not be discussed at any other time. The actual content of what is said may be purely confidential between the social care worker and the person concerned but may give the carer insight into aspects of the service user's personality, history and needs which were not apparent at other times.

May used to turn the bath into her reminiscence session and, away from listening ears, would relate all kinds of memories about her past life and work to her care worker. This helped her care worker to build up a relationship with May and gave her an understanding of May's need for reminiscence and extra time in the bath. The bath was something her care worker learned to take slowly, knowing that the bath was not just about getting May clean.

Use of photographs and pictures

Looking through photographs and/or magazines can often stimulate discussion about needs, contacts and issues which it may otherwise be difficult to discuss. This may be particularly the case with service users who find communication difficult or who have very few communication skills. Julie, who has learning difficulties and lives in a hostel, was able to contribute to her assessment by pointing to photographs of people with whom she likes to spend time, of activities she likes doing and places she likes to go. Through the use of magazine pictures she could show how she would like her room and the foods she likes to eat.

All of the above tools can be used towards an assessment, which can be concluded with a summary of needs. This in turn provides the basis upon which a care plan can be formulated.

Care planning and care agreements

Assessment and care planning are so inter-related that a great deal has already been said about care planning. From assessments arise care plans and from the implementation of care plans arise revised

assessments. A great deal of thought, discussion and consultation with the service user, carers and others involved in the user's network needs to take place in order that an optimum care plan is achieved. The term 'care plan' is the term most often used by agencies, but the term 'care agreement', discussed by Brearley (1977), has great relevance to social care. The result of an assessment should be an agreement with the service user about how needs are to be met, how problems can be dealt with and how an optimum quality of life can be achieved as a result of the assessment. This is the care plan. Brearley, in writing about care agreements states:

> People enter residential care because they are in need of help with personal care tasks which they cannot manage themselves . . . A first stage in settling in should therefore be to bring together the previous assessment and objectives set before admission with growing understanding of the residential staff in order to plan for the best way to provide care. It is most appropriate to think of this as a 'Care Agreement' to be reached between the Home and the resident . . .

The dominant philosophy of community care has perhaps dated the above statement a little but not much. It may now be a care agreement between the service user and the social services or the social work department; admission is unlikely to be seen initially as something permanent but as a period of assessment. However, the idea of a care agreement in order to plan for the best way to provide care is as relevant as it ever was.

Important points about care planning

From discussions with social care workers the following points emerge as important in care planning:

1) Involve and empower the service user as much as possible in negotiating an agreed plan.

2) The care plan should be written down. This seems obvious but it is not always done. A keyworker and service user may carry round a plan in their heads and assume that everyone else knows what it is. If there is a plan of care it needs to be used consistently by everyone involved in the care of the service user.

3) Be specific about how the care plan is to be achieved and who is going to do what.

4) Distinguish, if possible, what it is hoped to achieve in the short term and the long term.

5) Before a care plan can be developed there is a need for the people contributing to and co-ordinating the plan to gain the service user's trust and confidence.

6) A review/re-evaluation procedure should be built into planning.

7) Try to make the planning process non-threatening and informal.

8) A care plan should arise from the presentation of real choice, and maximum information should be provided about the choices available. There should be honesty where little or no choice is possible.

9) If the service user requires help in reaching decisions in relation to planning it may be useful for him or her to be present with an independent advocate. A social care worker can be a source of both information and advocacy.

10) There are no absolutes about care planning; there is no one best care plan which can be uniformly applicable. Each agency will establish the best way of care planning for service users.

Care planning and resources

Sadly, even with emphasis upon needs-led assessment, it is not possible to put into effect a totally needs-led approach to care planning. The unfortunate practical issue of resources rears its head and demands consideration. This does not mean that resources should be the guiding star in deciding what can and cannot be included in a care plan; if resources are not at present available it is worth putting up a fight and presenting a well researched and reasoned case to obtain them. However, planning must take into account what is likely to be possible and resources are among the factors to be taken into account. Melanie Henwood (1995) states that towards the end of 1994 financial pressure on local authority social services departments increased, with real fears of authorities running out of money. Against this background resources have to become a consideration.

What is meant by resources? Money, of course, is one resource. Other resources include services, staff time, activities, anything which may be needed to fulfil the care plan. Two very positive things which the 1990 legislation did in relation to resources was to provide flexibility in how money could be spent and to ringfence money for certain groups i.e. the government set aside certain sums of money to be used only for certain groups, including people with mental health problems, alcohol or drugs-related problems, HIV and AIDS. This flexibility means that money can be used for community care, residential care or both, and means that care plans can now cross boundaries which had previously been almost impossible to cross. Unfortunately, the problem of distinguishing between what is health care and what is not remains contentious, though joint/collaborative funding goes some way towards dealing with this problem.

Full and partial care plans

As with assessments, care plans may present the whole picture or may apply only to a particular section of the service user's life. The main care plan should influence partial plans and vice versa. Below is an example of a care plan produced by a social care student on placement in a hospice and a service user, Philomena Macdonald. This relates to the ways in which the needs can be met within the hospice setting. Other plans may relate to specific activities or to the total plan of care for the service user in his or her situation.

CASE EXAMPLE – PHILOMENA

Philomena Macdonald (her real name) has given permission for her care plan to be reproduced in the hope that other people are encouraged to say what they would like from their carers, especially if, like Philomena, they are in a physically very dependent situation. Before producing the plan there is included some background information about Mrs Macdonald so that the plan can be seen in context.

Philomena Macdonald is approaching 60 years' old, formerly a teacher of languages. She and her husband have seven children. Eleven years ago she was diagnosed as suffering from motor neurone disease. This disease is a particularly debilitating one which is progressive and for which there is not at present any cure. It has deprived Philomena of most of her movement, making it impossible for her to attend to her own needs, and most of her speech, though she can be understood by those who persevere. She still has a very active mind and writes poetry by dictating through lip movements to one of her daughters.

The care plan

Philomena's Morning Routine

Before I get out of bed, put on my socks and shoes, making sure my toes are straight, then put my collar on.

Lifting out of bed – two helpers

To get me in a sitting position with my legs over the bed edge, the first helper supporting my back brings the top part of my body forward. At the same time the second helper brings my legs over the bed edge. This must be done at the same time because if my legs come off the bed first it's very painful for me. Check with me to see if I'm near enough the edge of the bed before lifting me for the commode. Place my turning board a few inches from the bed, and place my feet in position on top of disc. Check with me first to see if everything is OK for lifting.

(The plan goes on to a detailed account of commode, eye and nose care and then proceeds to breakfast.)

Breakfast

Bowl of porridge
Five Alive × 2 Hot water
Pot of tea × 2 Black no sugar
20 mls lactulose

Place towel across shoulders, place napkin on top of towel. Fold strip of white roll and wrap it around my left hand, keeping my thumb and fingers together. Put half juice and water in a cup with half the lactulose. Place cup in my left hand and supporting wrist raises cup to my mouth. I will blink when I need a rest, in the event of which you put the palm of your hand on my forehead and push my head back gently on to my pillow. Repeat this until I have finished then repeat with second cup the same as the first.

When finished I will take porridge, stopping in between for sips of tea. I will blink my eyes when I want to change from eating to drinking or vice versa. If my tea is too hot, pour from cup to cup to cool it down. Do not wipe my lips; dab with a tissue when needed. When I'm finished remove towel and put my shawl on, put my collar on, sort my pillow and put my head back. While I'm waiting for my bath put my radio on. I will let you know what station I require.

The plan continues with a bath, lunch and so on through the day. Philomena also emphasises the she likes people to talk to her and that she has not lost her head just because she can hardly move or speak.

The care plan is pinned to her wardrobe so that all care workers can see it and there is consistency of care. It is a care plan which applies to day to day care and in this sense is only a partial plan, though in Philomena's case there are no plans for major change. The main objectives are to maintain the present situation, maximising Philomena's say about how she would like to be treated, maximising her comfort and enabling her to feel as secure as possible so that she can enjoy life as much as possible – and she still does appreciate life and has a great deal to give as well as to receive.

This plan places the ball very much in the service user's court and demonstrates too the ways in which social care worker roles often demand a whole variety of skills. In this case they involved working closely with other members of the care team since some but certainly not all, of Philomena's needs are medical ones. A social care student working with her suggested this shared care plan, taking account of a broad range of needs and not limited by a medical model or concentration upon physical needs. Thankfully, there are moves towards a more holistic approach to care, especially within the hospice movement and in training, but observations made by students in 1996 indicate that in many settings movement is rather on the slow side.

Exercise 2

Choose someone with whom you work closely (or if this is not possible, from your imagination). Co-ordinate and write an assessment and care plan which:

- gives a brief description of the service user in order to place him or her in context

- states what tools you will use in the assessment

- gives a timescale for the assessment/care planning process

- provides a summary of needs

- provides a plan of care, distinguishing between what is to be achieved in the long and short term

- gives an indication of who is going to do what in this process.

This exercise can be extended, once you have read Chapters 7 and 8, to stating how the plan is to be implemented.

Suggestions for further reading

- Coulshed, V. (1991) *Social Work Practice*, 2nd edn, London: Macmillan.

  A gem of a book which has relevance for those working in social care settings; written in straightforward, comprehensible language with good use of examples.

- Seed, P. and Kaye, G. (1994) *Handbook for Assessing and Managing Care in the Community*. London: Jessica Kingsley.

  Although based upon research with people with learning difficulties, this book has a much wider application and is a well structured and interesting account, especially of the assessment process.

Implementing care plans

Social care workers seek to understand the needs and aspirations of each individual to bring them quality of life in ways which will enhance their independence as well as their interdependence. They then work to enable this to happen in ways which are appropriate to the individual.

Social Care Association, *The Social Care Task*, March 1993.

Implementation is carrying out what has been specified in the care plan, enabling the care plan to happen. There are many approaches to implementing plans, most of which can be incorporated into the care environment approach outlined in Chapter 8. This chapter and the following one are very much linked with one another and it was difficult to decide which one to put first. In this chapter some theoretical approaches are introduced which have been tried and tested and which will give you some useful tools in implementing plans. These ways of working come with various warnings and safeguards. The primary one is that respect for the service user and the improvement of his or her quality of life are the only justifications for using these approaches. Supervision, collaboration and support from other team members are important in their implementation. Implementation is part of a planned model of care shared with the service user, family members and other members of the care team. There should be built in monitoring and review. One mode of implementation, the use of communication and counselling skills, has already been discussed. Some other methods which may be useful in

implementing care plans are outlined below.

Behavioural work

The beauty of behavioural work is its simplicity and the fact that many social care workers use it already without really realising it. The reason for including it here is that it can be a very useful way to help people in social care settings to alter their behaviour and/or thought patterns so that they can operate in ways which are both more personally satisfying and more acceptable to others.

The theory of behavioural work is often surrounded by a good deal of jargon, so I have attempted to explain it in a way which is comprehensible not only to academic high flyers but also to ordinary mortals who have to apply the theory in a very practical way.

Behavioural work has its origins in learning theory, and rests upon the premise that a great deal of behaviour and the way we think and feel are learned. If behaviour and thinking seem to be reducing rather than enhancing quality of life then it may be a good idea to assist the service user towards quality-of-life-enhancing behaviours and thoughts. What has been learned can be unlearned and something else, more appropriate and satisfying and fulfilling, can replace what was there before. Alternatively, if behaviour has not already been learned for a situation, a new way of behaving can be learned. This can all be done by reinforcing or rewarding behaviours and/or thoughts which are beneficial, and ignoring and not rewarding other behaviours and thoughts. The theory is a little more complex than this, as will become evident below, but this is its essence. For the purposes of this discussion I have taken four strands of learning theory which can be used separately or in combination with one another.

Strand 1 – Pavlov's dogs

The first strand began its life in some experiments which Ivan Pavlov, a Russian professor of physiology in the 1920s, conducted on dogs: Pavlov's dogs. Many people have heard of Pavlov and his dogs without quite knowing what they did, why they are so famous and what on earth they have to do with social care practice. When the experiment is described you may begin to see why they have some relevance to what social care workers do, though not as much relevance as the second strand of learning theory which is described below.

1) Dogs salivate when they see food in their bowls (unconditioned response to unconditioned stimulus).

2) Food is given at the same time as a noise on a tuning fork (food, the unconditioned response, is associated with a tuning fork, the conditioned stimulus).

3) Dogs begin to associate the noise of a tuning fork with food (conditioned stimulus, the tuning fork, is associated with unconditioned stimulus, food).

4) Dogs soon salivate when they hear a tuning fork, even in the absence of food (conditioned response, salivation, to a conditioned stimulus, a tuning fork).

Initially, salivation was what in the theory is called an unconditioned response to an unconditioned stimulus, food; but salivation to the sound of a tuning fork was a conditioned response to a conditioned stimulus, the tuning fork. People too can develop conditioned responses to conditioned stimuli.

CASE EXAMPLE – JULIE

Julie was attacked one day on her way to school when she was hit by a bigger girl. She tried to hit back but friends of the bigger girl joined in and Julie was hurt. She now associates walking to school with being hit and walking to school with school. She therefore refuses to go to school, any school. Fear, an unconditioned response to an unconditioned stimulus (being attacked), has become refusal to go to school, a conditioned response (school refusal) to a conditioned stimulus (school). The behaviour to be unlearned is that all attendance at school is harmful and the behaviour to be learned is that school can be an enjoyable, fulfilling experience.

Some practical issues have to be dealt with here first so that the danger of going to school can be diminished. The source of bullying needs to be stopped which could be by removing the bully (not always possible), working with the bully to change behaviour (also not always possible) or by Julie changing schools (should not be necessary but may be a possible solution). Julie has to be enabled to relax on her way to school. This may be through a supportive adult going with her or through ensuring that she walks to school with a group of children or another child whom she likes. Very gradually the conditioned response to the conditioned stimulus can be extinguished. In the same way, using the example of Pavlov's dogs, if you stop giving food at the same time as sounding a tuning fork and sound a tuning fork with no accompanying food for long enough then salivation to the sound of a tuning fork will eventually die out. Behavioural techniques can be used in extinguishing unhelpful conditioned responses to conditioned stimuli.

Strand 2 – consequences

A lot of behaviour occurs because it is found to have desirable consequences. An example of this was given to me recently.

CASE EXAMPLE – ALAN

Alan, 14 years' old and living in a children's home, was creating havoc every time he did not get to see the programme he wanted on television. He would scream and shout and threaten to throw things. For the sake of peace a situation had developed where, for the most part, he got his way. Both staff and other children were colluding in this because they were afraid of trouble. So Alan learned that if he screamed and shouted he was allowed to watch the programme he wanted on the television, and whenever he did not get his way he screamed and shouted until he did. People did not really realise that they were reinforcing his antisocial behaviour. They found they got half an hour of peace if they let him watch his programme and, in the short term, half an hour of peace was very nice.

In looking at this in behavioural terms it is useful to use a model called the ABC model developed by Hudson and Macdonald (1986): 'A' stands for Antecedents which occur before the behaviour, 'B' stands for Behaviour and 'C' stands for Consequences. In examining Alan and his television watching, Figure 7.1 illustrates the model:

Antecedents	Behaviour	Consequences
Alan does not get the programme he wants on television.	Screams, shouts, threatens to throw things.	Allowed to see the programme he wants

Figure 7.1: The ABC model

In Alan's assessment, among the needs which had been identified and with which Alan himself had agreed, were the need to have more positive relationships with members of his peer group and family, and the need to gain control over his emotional outbursts in order to do this. The behaviour which was being reinforced in the children's home was in direct opposition to this and must be changed if the assessment is to have any meaning. The consequence of Alan's screaming and shouting should not be a positive reward – so what should it be?

In behavioural work the most effective way to deal with negative behaviour has been found to be to ignore it and to reward positive behaviour straight away and on a consistent basis. Everyone involved in working with the service user is involved in the programme and everyone responds in the same or a similar way in the event of undesirable behaviour and desirable behaviour. The rewards may be concrete things, something the service user enjoys doing or eating (remembering, however, healthy eating and the detrimental effects of sweets on teeth) and smiles and praise. Star charts may be useful here, where a star on a chart is given every time there is desirable behaviour. The star is accompanied by the obvious pleasure of the worker in terms of a smile and a 'well done'. Ten stars can mean a concrete reward in terms of watching a desired television programme or a treat which is known to be valued by the service user.

With complex tasks the task can be broken down into a series of much simpler steps in a process known as 'chaining'. The links in the chain eventually lead to the completion of the whole task. Initially, just one part of the task is rewarded: see Tom's case example.

The use of reward for desired behaviour and the ignoring of undesired behaviour comes with a word of warning. The outcome is not usually immediate and there is usually an escalation in the undesirable behaviour before it begins to diminish and eventually die out. Julie, a child of five living in a children's home, always got up again after going to bed. She liked to join in the adult evening and made a terrible fuss if she was put back to bed. Staff at the home made a record of Julie's behaviour over a two-week period and found that this was the most difficult aspect of her behaviour to deal with. They devised a programme whereby they would

CASE EXAMPLE – TOM

This example looks at enabling Tom, who has learning difficulties, to dress himself. He is 21 years' old and has always been helped to dress by his mother, out of kindness to him because he found dressing difficult and slow. However, attendance at a day centre has demonstrated to him and to his mother that he is capable of far more than he has previously attained and Tom is now eager to learn new skills. His mother, at first a reluctant accomplice, has now realised that this could help both of them, especially as she gets older and is less able to give physical assistance. Both she and the workers at the centre, together with Tom, have devised a programme whereby Tom will eventually be able to dress himself completely. The programme starts from the outside in, with Tom initially putting on his own coat, and then doing up the buttons and so on. Putting on his coat is initially rewarded and praised, then only when he does up the buttons as well does he get praise, and so on.

ignore Julie's demands to get up and firmly but kindly put her back to bed if she got up after bed time. In the morning they would offer praise and a treat if Julie had gone to bed quietly. At first her screams and shouts increased for several nights when she was not allowed to stay up. There was much gritting of teeth among staff, and other children in the home were given an explanation of what staff were trying to do. Just to make matters worse another two children decided to join Julie in her screaming and shouting. Eventually after two weeks of great difficulty, ignoring the undesirable behaviour worked and there was peace at bed time. Julie and the other children realised that they were not going to get their way and that they got a story and hugs and cuddles in the morning when they did not misbehave at night. However, it did take perseverance, consistent behaviour by all members of staff and the co-operation of older children in the home who also had a vested interest in having an uninterrupted evening.

Exercise 1

As a useful exercise in applying this theory:

1) Devise a behavioural programme for Alan which you think will enable him to have more positive relationships.

2) Think of rewards which may be appropriate to Tom in his dressing programme.

3) Plan a programme, using behavioural work, for a service user with whom you are working.

Strand 3 – models

Another strand of learning theory is that people can learn from others through their example. This is called modelling and social care workers can act as models of desired behaviour for service users. They can model such behaviour as staying calm in a crisis, not swearing, sitting down to eat a meal calmly and pleasantly at a table.

This part of the theory can also be put into operation through role play. The game is that the service user has to act the desired behaviour as demonstrated by the social carer. This kind of learning works best when a good relationship already exists. This may be enhanced, for instance, if children see adults from their own cultural background in positions of responsibility and trust.

Strand 4 – thoughts and feelings

Not only is behaviour learned, but ways of thinking and feeling may also have been learned. This strand of behavioural work is mostly about encouraging people who have come to think negatively about themselves, resulting in low self esteem and a negative self image, to see themselves in a more positive light, and to see their strengths rather than their weaknesses. It is often thought to be treading on rather dangerous ground to discuss working with people's thoughts, and so it is, but as long as the aim is kept positive, such work may change the whole way a person looks at him or herself and at life. People may, over a period of time, have come to think of themselves as worthless, or they may be dominated by such thoughts as 'I ought to do this, I must do that' when this is totally inappropriate or impossible, and feel guilty if they do not do these things. These negative ways of thinking can be very damaging to a person's feeling of well-being. It is possible to alter the way people think about themselves within behavioural work. Thinking and behaviour usually go hand in hand and changing one may also change the other.

Here are some things which service users have said about themselves:

- *'I am worthless. I can't do anything.'* This is an example of black and white, all or nothing thinking. It also often indicates labelling oneself as a hopeless failure when there were circumstances with which it was difficult to deal in any other way.

- *'I ought to have been there when it happened.'* This shows guilty thinking. It also shows how sometimes people personalise things as their fault when they could not possibly have been to blame. Care workers sometimes do this when they blame themselves for the behaviour of service users when they either were not there, or were there but the behaviour had little to do with the current situation.

- *'I had a terrible marriage. This shows I can't make relationships.'* This illustrates over-generalisation, assuming that one bad relationship will necessarily lead to others. It may also show how sometimes people remember only the bad and forget the good. A terrible marriage may not have started off that way, but remembering it only as terrible rules out the possibility of recalling the good parts when the relationship was successful. Someone making this kind of statement may also be seeing him or herself as a failure, when a set of circumstances and other people contributed to the breakdown.

- *'I know I won't like it there.'* This example shows how some people jump to conclusions without giving whatever it is a try. This is quite understandable, especially if they have had bad experiences in the past, but may be resolved if talked through and are given encouragement and support.

The idea that thoughts are amenable to change, and that people can be enabled to see the world through new eyes by altering set negative or harmful patterns of thought has been used in work with offenders. The method of working using a behavioural approach is called critical incident analysis. This focuses on the use of thinking and feeling – that is, cognitive skills – in order to increase the offender's knowledge and understanding of his or her behaviour, to increase awareness of the victim and awareness of how anger was used and managed; see Bob's case example.

This has, of necessity, been only a brief introduction to behavioural work. There is a lot of very good literature which will expand your knowledge of this field, and workers who feel that this may be useful

CASE EXAMPLE – BOB

A social care student working with an offender, fictionally called Bob, used this approach to enable Bob to understand the interplay between thoughts, feelings and actions. The student used knowledge of Bob's current and previous offences, witness statements and prosecution evidence, which she was given permission to see, to give a detailed picture of events. Bob also expressed his own version of events and their importance to him. This enabled him to feel recognised and valued as an individual and was also necessary for the analysis, showing how the service user receives and integrates information about the social world and how this information affects behaviour.

Bob was seen weekly by the worker for 12 weeks. During this time he was enabled to look at his way of thinking and how his thoughts about particular incidents triggered offending behaviour. He has rehearsed how he could have thought and acted differently and non-criminally in relation to particular incidents and he has been enabled to appreciate the effect his actions had upon his victims. Bob made several attempts to distort how events took place which required confrontation and negotiation from the worker whereby she would suggest another version of events, drawing material from other sources such as witness statements. The end result was that Bob was able to gain different perspectives of events, thoughts and feelings leading to and during incidents which had subsequently resulted in him being penalised. This was not an easy process and rested upon several features:

- Bob wanted to change
- the worker and Bob had a good working relationship
- the worker showed respect for Bob and worked at his own pace
- thoughts and feelings were regarded as being as important as action
- the implementation was preceded by careful assessment and planning
- the worker encouraged and praised Bob when he showed an ability to see his offending behaviour from another perspective

with some service users should read further and, if possible, obtain some training. Works particularly recommended are Hudson and Macdonald, 1986; Ainsworth and Fulcher, 1981; Coulshed, 1991; and Lishman, 1991.

Behavioural work has been developed and combined with other methods of working in coping with some particularly difficult situations faced by the social care worker. Gentle teaching (McGee, 1990) is used as an approach in dealing with challenging behaviour in the field of learning disability. It rests upon four main techniques:

- *ignore* the behaviour but stay with the person

- *interrupt* behaviours which are injurious or disruptive

- *re-direct* and focus attention on another activity

- *reward* the activity to which the person has been re-directed

People should be talked to warmly and quietly and their name used gently and positively. These techniques rest directly upon learning theory but have been developed for work with a particular group of people.

Therapeutic crisis intervention is currently receiving a lot of attention in work with young people in efforts to find satisfactory ways of dealing with very challenging behaviour. Again, it rests to some extent upon ideas gained from learning theory in combination with special holding techniques, knowledge of crises emphasising the importance of immediate response, and counselling techniques. Caplan (1961) observed:

During the period of upset of a crisis, a person is more susceptible to being influenced by others than at times of relative psychological equilibrium . . . this is a matter of supreme importance, because by deploying helping services to deal with individuals in crisis, a small amount of effort leads to a maximum amount of lasting response.

The use of any method of implementation, whether it is behavioural work, counselling or something else, is more likely during the period of crisis to have a 'maximum amount of lasting response'. Both gentle teaching and therapeutic crisis intervention require special training which is becoming increasingly available in the field of social care.

Task-centred work

Task-centred work has been found to be useful where there are:

- conflicts between or among people

- difficulties with social relationships

- difficulties in dealing with large organisations

- needs to develop certain skills

- problems of transition from one life stage to another

- situations where there are inadequate resources

- behavioural problems

It is not suitable for dealing with all problems or all people. Coulshed (1991) states in relation to research into the approach in a social services department in Buckinghamshire:

Those with a need for practical resources who acknowledged that they had a problem fared best. Involuntary/unwilling clients or those who had chronic, complex problems were less amenable.

Among the authors who have researched and developed ideas about task-centred work are Reid and Epstein (1977) who concluded that focused help, given at the right time can be as effective as long-term work.

The approach consists of the following steps:

1) An assessment with the service user of needs/problems.

2) Identifying tasks which need to be achieved in order to satisfy need.

3) Identifying and agreeing upon a particular task which it is important to achieve and which is realistically achievable.

4) Making up an agreement about how the task is to be achieved and when it is to be achieved by, with specific jobs associated with overall completion of the task. *Timescales* are especially important in this approach and it should be emphasised that any agreement is *always* within time limits, even though these may need to be reviewed at a later stage.

5) Sticking to the agreement with monitoring, encouragement and reinforcement from the social care worker.

6) Evaluating the situation at the end of the agreed time and reinforcing with the service user what has been achieved.

There are many advantages to such an approach from both the worker's and the service user's point of view:

• it does not take up vast amounts of time

• the aim is always known and in sight

• there is strong research evidence (Reid and Epstein) to suggest that this method has a good success rate which can be better than working with a service user on a long-term basis

• it motivates people to solve other problems in a similar way

• it increases the service user's ability to cope independently of the worker in the future.

In social care the achievement of the task is likely to be one aspect in continuing work but can have spin-offs in raising self esteem and providing encouragement towards a more fulfilling and creative life style; see Claire's case example on p. 86.

Developing networks

The usefulness of networks has already been demonstrated in the assessment process. They can, however, also play a role in implementation. The service user's network can be examined to see if there is potential for improvement or development

CASE EXAMPLE – CLAIRE

Claire is 25 years' old, lives in a hostel and has cerebral palsy. She has some degree of learning difficulty and is mobile with the aid of a wheelchair. Following a detailed assessment one identified need was that Claire wished to improve her literacy skills, particularly her ability to use a computer keyboard. This was part of a long-term aim to take some courses at a further education college. She and her keyworker (fortunately computer literate) devised a programme, based upon the use of a task-centred approach, to improve Claire's keyboard skills and expand her vocabulary. Previous attempts at this, which had been unspecific about what was to be achieved in what amount of time, had been unsuccessful, partly because there was a fear of putting too much pressure on Claire. Her worker, however, sensed her enthusiasm and devised a programme, based upon a knowledge of her present degree of skill and literacy, which would enable Claire, in her own home surroundings, to achieve something she considered to be worthwhile.

The programme was as follows:

1) Claire and her worker drew up together a list of 30 words, and four simple sentences using those words, which Claire was going to learn to type on the computer.
2) The programme was to last 10 weeks.
3) Claire agreed to learn to type five new words each week.
4) After six weeks she would type two sentences a week.
5) After eight weeks she would practise all her words and the sentences for two weeks.

The programme worked. It worked because Claire was able to see the end, the task was within her capability, the list of words was suggested by her, the keyworker gave encouragement and made sure that Claire stuck to her programme and did not try to do too much too soon. This all sounds very straightforward and, of course, this is not always the case – sometimes illness intervenes in the middle and the time scale has to be renegotiated, sometimes the task is not as achievable as at first thought and it is necessary to make some adjustments. But on the whole it is worth the effort and the energy needed to put the programme together and to set time aside to give help and encouragement when needed. The increase in motivation to achieve new tasks is usually very beneficial. This approach gives the message that change and progress are possible and working to a deadline can inspire commitment.

---

in order to improve quality of life. Taking Philip Seed's work as a guideline (Seed, 1990), three dimensions of networks can be examined and subsequently worked on:

1) The network can be examined in terms of its features: how does the network compare with what is 'normal' and socially acceptable; what

are the strengths and weaknesses of the network?

2) What kind of network is it? Is it a dense network with people in the network in contact with one another or is it a loose network with just a few links?

3) The quality of the links and relationships in the network can be examined: what are the positive and negative influences; do the relationships raise or lower self esteem; is the service user satisfied with the nature of the links and relationships within his or her network?

Through an interpretation of these dimensions the service user and care worker can reach some decisions about the way forward in developing the potential of the network. All too often social care workers are presented with problems or shortcomings in networks and service users need some help both to interpret these and to take action to improve the situation. As an example of this I will firstly show the network of Jim who is at present staying in Fernlea Children's Home (Figure 7.2, p. 88).

Initially, Jim's network was rather sparse and did not maximise its potential. All three aspects of the network were worked on with Jim in order to improve his quality of life – its features, density and quality all received attention – and after considerable work from Jim himself, his keyworker, social worker, other members of the care team and Jim's family, Jim's network ended up as in Figure 7.3, p. 89.

The second example shows the network of Ted, who has just gone to live in a core and cluster project after spending many years on a long-stay psychiatric ward in a large hospital.

From Figure 7.4 (p. 90) it can be seen that Ted does have social contacts, especially through his weekday attendance at a day centre; also he visits his brother once a week on the bus and he goes to the pub once a week with his social worker who intends to close his case within the next few weeks because he feels that Ted is doing so well. Ted is quite upset about this and also points out in his diary that he often feels lonely in the evenings, often thinks of two friends from the hospital whom he no longer sees and would also like his brother to come to see him sometimes instead of him always trailing out to see his brother.

Exercise 2

What do you think can be developed in Ted's network? Draw another network diagram which you feel would give Ted a better quality of life and with which you think he would feel happier.

Once a network analysis has been undertaken it can be used as a base point for comparison in the future. A new network diagram can be drawn up, for example at the end of the year, and compared with the original. What has been achieved? Are there still areas which the service user would like to develop further? What will be the respective roles of the user, the worker and others in this?

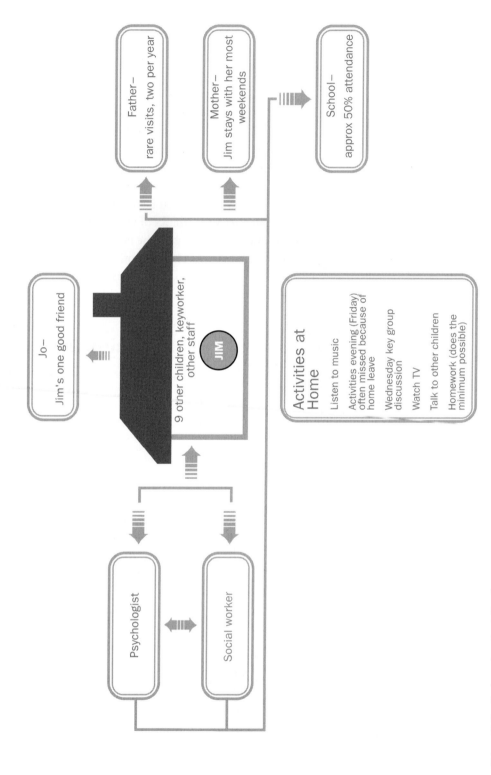

Figure 7.2: Jim's network at Fernlea

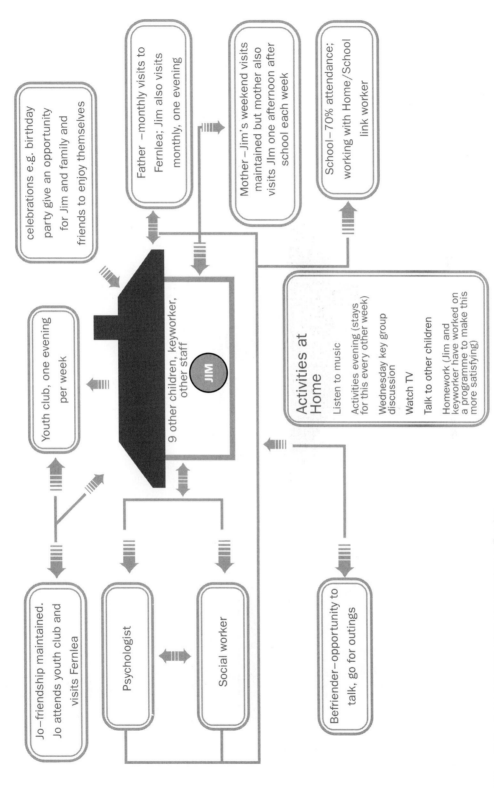

Figure 7.3: Jim's network after six months at Fernlea

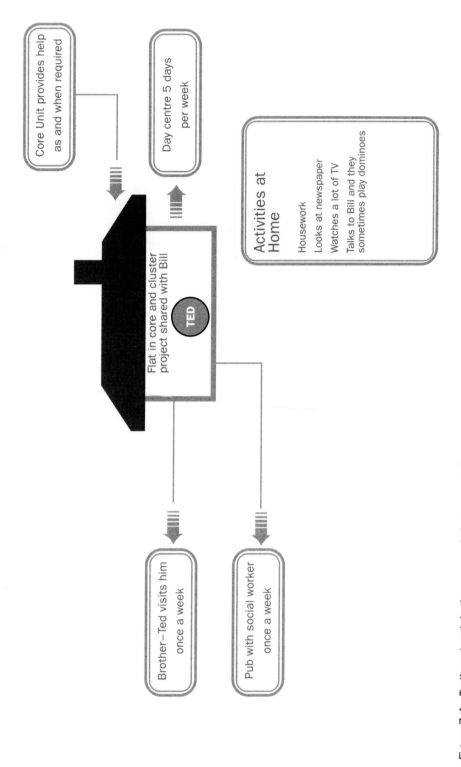

Figure 7.4: Ted's network in the core and cluster project

Advocacy

A further way in which social care workers can assist service users with the implementation of plans is through advocacy. Advocacy, in *Webster's Dictionary*, is when someone pleads the cause of another or speaks or writes in support of something. In social care it can also be the encouragement and provision of information to enable service users to advocate for themselves (self advocacy). Advocacy is not a new concept and, like community care, has gained additional emphasis in recent years. The growth of a citizen's advocacy movement, the need for many people with learning disabilities or mental illness for support to find the most fulfilling solution to their needs when being discharged from long-stay hospitals, and emphasis upon the concept in disability legislation, have given it a new prominence.

Advocacy can be seen as a form of empowerment for people who are unable to speak up for themselves or are prevented from doing so because of their marginalised position in society. It applies particularly to vulnerable groups such as people with learning disabilities, physical and/or sensory disabilities, mental health problems, to elderly people and abused children. Some members of these groups are perfectly able to advocate for themselves and should be encouraged to do so; it would be disempowering to provide advocacy where it was not needed. Others will need the support of someone to advocate on their behalf.

Among the many ways of looking at advocacy three are emphasised here: case advocacy and cause advocacy identified by Bull (1982), and internal advocacy identified by Patti (1971).

Case advocacy

This is perhaps the form of advocacy with which most people are familiar. It occurs when an advocate takes up a particular problem of the service user and argues on his or her behalf. For example, an advocate might argue the case for a person being discharged from a long-stay hospital to be allocated a place in a small community-based hostel. The process of advocacy in a situation like this often requires the advocate to fight the system, to be very persistent, to represent not his or her own viewpoint but that of the service user through empathy, looking at the world through the service user's eyes. When the service user has communication difficulties it may take a long time to build up a view of what he or she really wants, and the advocate has to be prepared to work at the relationship. Skills of communication, negotiation and mediation are vital.

Cause advocacy

This occurs when the advocate argues for changes to or reform of a system of administration or practice which causes difficulties or prevents the service user from optimising quality of life. For example, it used to be the case that people with a terminal illness had to go through a lengthy assessment before qualifying for disability living allowance or attendance allowance. They were often dead before the benefit arrived. Many of those working with people with terminal illness battled with the Department of Social Security for a change to the system and this eventually occurred so that now, with the signature of his or her GP, a person with a terminal illness can receive the appropriate benefit almost immediately. Case advocacy and cause advocacy are related in that changes to one will have an impact upon the other. Arguing individual cases can promote the cause of a particular group, and arguing a cause can improve the lot of individuals.

Internal advocacy

This aims to change the policies, programmes or procedures of an agency from the inside and may be initiated by employees in relation to their own employing agency. It is undertaken where the agency does not seem to be maximising its effectiveness in terms of fulfilling need. This does present some obvious problems for social care workers setting out to change their own agencies. They may be seen as threatening and presumptuous, or they may be seen as showing imagination and initiative. This depends on how the subject is tackled, how secure the leadership is and how well the team is functioning as a team. All of these things need to be considered before internal advocacy is attempted, although, given the 'right' circumstances, it can be a very effective way of helping a large number of service users with their problems.

An example of internal advocacy was the gradual introduction of outings and activities into the programme in a home for people with dementia, which was first suggested by a social care worker at a team hand-over meeting. Eventually, activities became part of the culture of the home. Social care workers demonstrated the potential for these and their inclusion became part of agency policy.

In all of the above senses social care workers can take on advocacy roles, although sometimes they may not be the best people to do so. Limitations arise because:

- they are employees and can only work within their role and within agency policy, even though they may also be advocating to change these

- other duties may prevent there being enough time to give to advocating adequately on behalf of a service user

- some of the requirements for which a service user needs an advocate may be beyond the professional ability of the social care worker, for example where legal advocacy by a barrister, lawyer or solicitor is more appropriate. The growth of independent personal advocacy through citizen advocates goes some way towards filling the gaps which social care workers, social workers and other professionals are unable to fill.

Citizen advocacy

Citizen advocates are volunteers who become advocates for individuals who need representation and often a fairly substantial time commitment. They have the advantages of independence, and support and supervision from a co-ordinator. They often remain as advocate for the same partner over a period of years, developing a substantial helping relationship. Citizen advocates aim to represent the partner's views as vigorously as if they were their own. With the knowledge that this service exists, social care workers can refer service users to it where they think that this may be helpful.

In spite of limitations and the growth of citizen advocacy there still remains a potentially important role for social care workers in advocating for service users. Sometimes, especially if they are keyworkers, they are the people who know the service user best and can best represent his or her needs to the outside world, they can change things from within their agencies to improve the quality of life for all service users and they can promote self advocacy through the provision of information, support and the opportunity for service user groups to meet to discuss issues. The performance of the role of social care worker can itself be seen as a form of advocacy, sometimes called exemplary advocacy, where the worker aims to meet the real needs of service users and where people with difficulties are given every opportunity to live as normal a life as possible through the support of appropriate services.

Working with groups

> . . . what the group can achieve is largely dictated by the combined potential, abilities, experience, attitudes and relationships of the members and the leader . . . The more each individual is prepared to put into the group the more in fact he will receive from the group. (Douglas, 1978.)

Groups in social care settings are rather fluid things – people come and people go and few go on for ever. The same people who form groups often see each other at other times of the day and night, share meals, watch television, sit and chat and argue with one another. The groups may serve social, learning, activity or therapeutic functions or a mixture of these; they may be reminiscence groups, discussion groups, a residents' committee or groups for looking at relationships or a particular kind of problem such as offending or bereavement. Some groups

will be small with just a few attenders, others may include most members of an agency. So the variables of the group will be the people, the time, the place, the stability, the purpose, the leadership and the effects of things outside the group which impinge upon members. This all requires a degree of adaptability on the part of the social care worker working with groups in social care settings. Below are some of the traditional concepts associated with group work, though these should be interpreted in terms of the particular circumstances in which the worker finds him or herself.

Groups and groupings

In the excellent work *Groups and Groupings* (Brown and Clough, 1989) a group is defined as: 'a plurality of persons who have a common identity, at least some feeling of unity, and certain common goals and shared norms'.

Groups can be distinguished from groupings which are much less well defined collections of people who may well meet together, share some things in common but do not have the 'togetherness' of a group. Six people sitting in the lounge of a day centre all talking to one another do not constitute a group but a grouping. They have not met at a particular time in a particular place for a particular purpose; there is nothing which identifies them as a group sharing a goal or goals, though they may benefit from and enjoy the occasion.

However, a bereavement group which meets on Tuesday afternoons with the aim of enabling members to cope with a bereavement is a group. It exists through time for a purpose and although some leave and others join, there is some stability and a feeling of belonging among its members. Activity groups can be seen as either groups or groupings, often with features of both. If an activity group meets only once, for example, it is probably better defined as a grouping. If it meets weekly and develops an identity through time, it develops features of a group rather than a grouping, especially if members help one another, make mutual decisions and develop relationships within it. Where a group exists within a social care setting such as a day or residential unit, it will be affected by the life of the unit and will in its turn have an effect on the unit, all of which must be taken into account. Among the main reasons for looking at groups are that they can be an extremely effective way of assisting people to deal with some kinds of problem, ranging from relationship problems to dealing with other aspects of everyday life and that they can contribute substantially to improving the quality of life for service users in almost any social care setting.

Exercise 3

Look at your own place of work and distinguish groups from groupings. Make a list of features of:

• groups

• groupings.

Group stages

One helpful theory in understanding how groups form and develop is that of Tuckman (1965). He presents a theory of group stages. Although it is unlikely that a group will fit neatly into these stages, the model is helpful both in developing an understanding of what is going on and in providing pointers towards enabling the group to be optimally effective. These stages are forming, storming, norming, performing and ending. Each of these will be examined in turn.

Forming

As the title suggests, this is the stage at which the future shape of the group is determined and the group begins to form into something recognisable. At present the group is moving from being a grouping to a group. Some of the characteristics of this initial stage are:

• a dependence upon the group leader

• anxiety about being a group member

• individuals trying out approaches within the group i.e. trying to find their role in it and perhaps initially showing reluctance to take any responsibility without weighing up what this involves, what the responses of others will be and whether it is safe

There are various exercises which a group leader can use at this time in order to enable members to get to know one another. Ice breakers sometimes allay anxieties. For example, each group member can be given the task of introducing another group member after a short discussion with this person about his or her interests, or all group members can use an adjective to describe themselves e.g. 'cool Chris'. Group exercises can be used to encourage group discussion and participation. For example, group members can be set the task of deciding how they will survive on a desert island or, to borrow an exercise from NASA, how they will prioritise a list of objects to take to the moon.

Storming

This is the second stage in the group's formation and is as crucial as the first in deciding whether or not the group is a success. Individuals in the group are testing out at this stage, trying out different roles, seeking their own place within the group and sometimes competing with others for position. Again, leadership plays an important part. In this stage the leader's task is:

- to involve all group members in the task of the group and ensure that activities are both within the capability of group members and are not too threatening for them

- to be supportive to all group members in order that members can feel secure enough to participate, to confront difficult issues and test out their own positions and views

- to remain calm, collected, optimistic and show a will that the group will succeed

Norming

Forming and storming will probably still be going on at intervals throughout the life of any group, but as a group matures it progresses towards a stage of norming and away from the pressures of the first two stages. At this third stage the group is characterised by the development of trust and 'belongingness' among members, a feeling that this is *our* group in which there are 'norms' or accepted ways of doing things. This accepted way of doing things gives the group a culture and identity and members may feel freer and safer about expressing themselves.

The leader's task at this stage involves accepting that members now have a group feeling and may be more able to take on decision making and organisational tasks which were previously the leader's responsibility. The group leader should be able to withdraw a little from being the decision maker to being a more background figure; leading from behind, there when necessary but not obtrusive. The functioning of the group at this point will generally be increasingly concerned with relating its activities to the real world outside. This can be furthered through encouraging tasks which are to be achieved between group meetings.

Performing

This occurs when the group is actually doing what it set out to achieve for its members, accomplishing the aims and objectives which were set, with all members feeling that they have both a relevant part to play and that the group experience is of benefit. A discussion group set up to discuss family relationships will actually be doing this, with members feeling safe and confident to express their views and making suggestions for the direction the group is to take. The group should by now be reasonably self sufficient, with leadership necessary only when there is unreasonable conflict or the group seems to come to a stop and needs encouragement and reassurance to continue.

Ending

Most groups do come to an end. This end may have been determined beforehand: 10 sessions for a group of care leavers to discuss and make plans for their future; the task which the group set itself may have been achieved; or there just may seem to be no reason for the group to continue. Feelings associated with this ending may be some combination of sadness and loss, jubilation that what was aimed for has been achieved, flatness and disappointment if it is felt that not much has been gained. Sometimes groups try to delay ending by arranging one more meeting or they decide to have reunions, which means that the ending is not the final parting.

The task of the group leader at this stage is to help group members to cope with all the feelings surrounding the ending, to enable the group to assess the gains and the losses and to enable members to take forward into the future the idea of the group as a positive experience. An acknowledgement of ending, in the form of a special event such as an outing or a party, is often useful to round things off and to complete satisfactorily.

This theory of Tuckman's is useful in looking at how groups evolve and the stages in their development. These stages are not hard and fast and do not have distinct separations one from another; also groups, especially ones which do not have closed membership, can go backwards and forwards between stages. The usefulness of the theory lies in enabling social care workers to have some understanding of the tasks of leading and setting up a group and of what to expect if they do. A good deal of working with groups comes from experience and is assisted by training. Also, any group worker has to be adaptable to the group members, for example groups of people with dementia or learning

difficulties may demand much more of the leader than groups of adults with problems associated with bereavement who may eventually form a self help group without any formal leadership.

Advantages of working with groups

Some advantages of working with groups were mentioned when considering the assessment process – see the list on p 69. Here I use three examples of groups to illustrate the possible advantages of group work.

The reminiscence group

The first example is of a reminiscence group held in a home for people with dementia. The group meets weekly at a set time in the same room and has a varied programme. For example, on different occasions:

- members are encouraged to bring their own objects or photographs

- a reminiscence box is borrowed from the local museum

- someone comes in to show slides taken from old photographs of the area, of its industries, buildings and landmarks

- the reminiscence resource cupboard is used (this is a collection of relevant everyday objects and photographs which has been built up over the years, some of it contributed by service users)

What advantages does this group have over working with individuals on a one to one basis? Among the advantages are the following:

1) It is a social occasion and enables members to maintain or develop social skills.

2) The group is an event to look forward to.

3) Members are mainly of the same generation and will have memories in common which they can share.

4) The experience of the group can be looked back upon and shared afterwards; staff can encourage this for those who have difficulty remembering it.

5) Members can help others to remember things which they thought they had forgotten.

6) It can empower people with dementia, enabling them to communicate and to feel that their past has value. In this way self esteem can be raised.

An intermediate treatment project

As a second example I have taken the use of group work in an intermediate treatment project for young adults with a background of offending. This project is described by Lucy Ball and Theo Sowa in Brown and Clough, 1989. They worked with young offenders aged 14 17 who would otherwise have been given custodial sentences. Two groups of eight young people attended the project, initially on a full-time basis, Monday to Friday, 9.30 am to 4.00 pm (1.30 pm on Wednesdays). There was a formal group work programme, some individual work and some work in groupings. The formal group work had specific objectives, including to stop people from offending, to develop

self awareness about offending and to change offending patterns. Ball and Sowa see the major advantages of group work in this setting as empowering young people and helping them to take more control of their lives. They emphasise the need for regular evaluation in order that problems can be identified and dealt with. The usefulness of Tuckman's model is also acknowledged, though they emphasise the necessity for workers to use their own analyses of the group process and not use a particular stage as an excuse when things are not going well. 'Storming' can be an excuse, for example, for 'bad leadership, sloppy planning, external pressures on group members . . .' and appropriate action should be taken.

A bereavement group

The final example is a bereavement group in a hospice which I co-led with a colleague and which we ran with the help of some trained volunteers. This group, which was held every two weeks, had a fluid membership with people leaving and new people arriving all the time. The group's objective was to enable people to cope with loss, not to get stuck at a particular stage in the bereavement process and to achieve an improved level of adjustment, acceptance and emotional health. Some advantages of using a group approach were as follows:

• Group members could share experiences. On one occasion a woman related an out-of-body experience. She told group members how, when she first learned of her husband's death, she had gone out of the hospice and walked across a footbridge over the River Clyde . . . but she had actually felt as though she was floating outside her body and looking down on herself as someone very small and very sad. Other group members could relate to this and recounted similar experiences.

Another member told of how he had always regarded himself as a calm, sane and sensible person. But a few days after his wife's death he had felt that he was going completely mad. He had an urge to go out into the street and shout and scream at the top of his voice and to throw things. It was only with the greatest effort that he had prevented himself from doing this. Again, group members said that they had also felt themselves to be going mad and were reassured to discover that this 'madness', containing so much anger, frustration and sheer powerlessness to change what had happened, was for many people a normal part of the grieving process.

• Group members were very supportive of one another, sometimes in quite unexpected ways. In a group which had a very mixed age range, from early 20s to 80s, one of the most supportive members was a bereaved man in his 60s who took under his wing a woman in her 20s whose mother had died. He was able to offer her a lot of understanding and encouragement partly because his own daughters were experiencing many of the feelings which she was experiencing.

It often surprised me, although perhaps it should not have done, that many of the people who supported one another were of widely different ages and experiences of life and bereavement, and were themselves experiencing enormous difficulties and losses. One of the huge benefits of working with a group, any group, is the unexpected, surprising

outcome which sometimes seems like a small miracle which has only been made possible in this setting.

• In the group setting a lot of people could receive help from a limited number of experienced counsellors/group workers. This was a practical reality in a situation in which one to one counselling was in very limited supply and took up a large quantity of worker time. The group was not only a better way of fulfilling the needs of most people who were bereaved but it was also more economical. Additionally, it enabled the limited availability of one to one counselling to be given to those who needed it most, those who did not wish to go to the group sessions, or came and then could not handle them or felt that they were not yet ready for them.

• The group setting enabled people to work through the stages of grief to reach a healthy outcome.

• For many people attending the group it was the only social occasion at which they felt comfortable.

• It was a way for some group members to begin to adjust to their changed status e.g. from being a wife to being a widow.

• The group enabled some members to form new friendships.

• It became obvious after some months of running the group that for some members it was no longer needed as a way of coping with bereavement, but these members did not want to leave because the group still served a social function for them. As a result of this, a self help, self run group was formed by those members who had coped with bereavement and wanted a social life. This group met at a different time from the other group, arranged outings and activities and was there for those who had worked through loss to a stage of acceptance and readjustment.

These three different groups, the reminiscence group, the intermediate treatment group and the bereavement group, all in their way promoted the values of social care and focused a great deal upon empowering people to cope with life more effectively outside the group setting.

Exercise 4

Choose an opportunity to set up and run a group in your workplace. Plan how you will set about this, decide upon the goals and a timescale and present your ideas to a team meeting. After discussion with service users and team members implement the plan and evaluate how effective you think the group is in achieving its goals. This exercise could also be done in collaboration with a colleague who acts as co-worker.

Suggestions for further reading

- Brown, A. and Clough, R. (eds.) (1989) *Groups and Groupings, Life and Work in Day and Residential Centres*. London: Tavistock/Routledge.

A collection of papers written by experienced practitioners about a whole variety of work with groups and groupings in many different settings, ranging from small group homes to day centres.

- Coulshed, V. (1991) *Social Work Practice, An Introduction*, 2nd edn. London: Macmillan.

I have already mentioned this book but it is worth mentioning again. Coulshed provides summaries of many ways of implementing plans, with good examples.

- Tuckman, B.W. (1965) 'Developmental Sequences in Small Groups'. *Psychological Bulletin* 63 (6).

This article outlines the stages through which groups progress.

The care environment approach

Clothes, food and warmth are the most powerful means by which group practitioners convey care for the individual. By offering bodily comfort and guaranteeing personal space a practitioner converts caring into a nurturing experience for the individual, so providing the basis for later work of modifying attitudes and behaviour.

AINSWORTH AND FULCHER, 1981.

Children care about shabby, run-down buildings, lack of privacy in bedrooms, showers, toilets and bathrooms. They recognise them as indicators that they are undervalued and that their needs have been overlooked.

KAHAN, 1994.

Often, social care workers do not think of the environment in which they work as part of the plan of care and its implementation. In fact not only does the care environment act as the background to everything care workers do but can also be an integral part of the process of caring. Particularly in group care settings, such as residential homes and day centres, the care environment itself can be used, adjusted or altered to be part of the implementation process. It can be viewed as a resource and a mode of implementation in its own right. Four threads can be seen in this approach:

1) The physical environment, that is the building and grounds, their location, the things in them and the way they are maintained and adorned.

2) The organisational environment, including the way the organisation is run and managed.

3) The care maintenance and therapeutic environment, that is how the care environment can be utilised to provide a life for service users which is as fulfilling as possible.

4) The community environment which concentrates on links with families and the wider community.

These threads are inextricably intertwined

but for the purposes of discussion I have, of necessity, examined them separately.

Physical environment

Any care environment offers potential for both good and harm. One of the greatest dangers is that of institutionalisation, already discussed in Chapter 1. Planners and care workers should strive to create an environment which is free from institutionalising forces. In any kind of group care environment there is inevitably a stress between the needs of individuals for personal space, choice and individual expression and the needs of the agency to be well organised, hygienic, efficient and cost effective. Social care workers are responsible for maximising the former (as well as giving attention to the latter), for looking at the care environment in which they work and ensuring that it is predominantly keeping the needs of service users paramount. The physical environment plays a part in this.

The National Health Service and Community Care Act 1990 talks about providing *homely settings* in the community for those who are unable to live in their own homes. A homely setting is somewhere that feels like home. Among the things which count here are social care workers who are concerned about what the place looks like and feels like and who care about consulting the people who are living or spending their days in this environment. I worked for some years in a hospice where great consideration was given to the feel of the physical environment: the décor, the furniture, the curtains, the bedcovers and the cups and saucers. Some of this takes money, but it is not just money – it is also about enabling service users to choose things which they would like to have around them or, if they are not able to make such choices, helping them as far as is humanly possible to live in an environment which satisfies their needs and enhances their feeling of well-being. This means getting away from the same bedcovers for everyone, the same cream paint in every single room, bare cold floors because they are easy to clean. Some of the things which I have seen recently which have enhanced the physical environment are as follows:

In a home for people with dementia

- a warm, welcoming, carpeted entrance area (the smile and warm welcome from the receiving social care worker also helped)

- attractive, well framed pictures on the walls of corridors and rooms, some of them contributed by service users, relatives or local artists

- a colourful, much used garden with garden seats

- recognisable pictures chosen by service users – as well as names – on room doors so that they were instantly recognisable

- photographs of staff in a strategic place in the home

- items of furniture brought from former homes by service users

- a predominance of single rooms

- a tea room which service users helped to run for the benefit of themselves, their relatives and friends

- one man's friendly dog

- a cupboard full of items which could be used in reminiscence sessions: old photographs, clothes, household items etc.

In a children's home

- murals painted by the children and staff in the main lounge/play room

- a play area free from the need to be careful with the furniture and with enough space for some physical activity

- a cosy room where children could take family members and other visitors

- enough computers, books and play equipment for all children to be able to find something constructive and creative to do in their spare time

- sturdy, challenging play equipment in the grounds

Organisational environment

As important as the physical environment is the way an organisation is run and managed. The following are among the organisational factors which contribute to a positive care environment.

Clear philosophy, aims and objectives

All staff should be given some guidance by those in responsible positions about what their organisation is striving for, what ideas guide the thinking behind the care which is provided and what the end result of all the work and thought should be. Some

agencies have set this out very clearly for everyone to read; others seem never to have thought about it, except perhaps in terms of aiming to make ends meet or make a profit. Below I reproduce two statements by organisations which encompass their philosophy. These should be read critically by readers and adapted to meet the needs of their own agencies. The first statement is from a residential school for boys and is headed 'General Philosophy of Child Care'.

The general approach to Child Care is eclectic with an emphasis on positive reinforcement and encouragement. Within a living and working environment children are given a modern therapeutic environment in which to live, grow and develop. Boundaries are set in terms of socially acceptable behaviour and in general children are encouraged to adopt a set of values and expectations that will serve them well at home, school and in the community. Whereas an understanding and accepting approach is used this is augmented with rules and an underlying behaviour modification strategy to enable the individual child to respond within his own concept level and time frame.

Behaviours which are seen to be situation specific are dealt with within that specific situation. Although there will always be exceptions it is felt that there should be no carry over or spin-off from one situation to another. For example, poor behaviour in the classroom does not, in the normal course of events, affect say, access to recreational resources or home visits, but must be addressed within the classroom.

Care practice . . . is seen as 'normalised' in that what goes on may be held by parents as good parenting and by children as right and proper. Ultimately the goal is to engender within the child a set of acceptable behaviours such that he is able to achieve his own personal targets and hopefully leave school with the expectation of having employment and a pleasant post 16 life.

Through the use of a Care and Support Plan developed for each child and his special difficulties it is hoped to set personal and attainable goals and targets that provide each child with a framework for development. It is important that any progress made by a pupil is not undermined by negative behaviours.

There is no mincing of words there. The second example is set out as a residents' charter in a residential and nursing home for elderly people. This is handed to clients and staff, with a further copy framed and hung in the entrance hall:

Residents . . . have the right to:

1) *dignity; to respect by staff of all beliefs and choices of lifestyle and in all circumstances*
2) *kindness*
3) *privacy*
4) *confidentiality in all matters, personal and medical and protection of interests, social and legal*
5) *freedom of movement and activity, subject only to safety*
6) *freedom of choice, so far as is practicable*
7) *a homely and safe environment*
8) *feel and be treated as a valued member of the small community of the . . . Home*
9) *have visitors whenever and wherever wanted*
10) *associate with others and build up relationships, both inside and outside the Home*
11) *have spiritual, emotional and physical needs respected and met*
12) *a high standard of care, be given details of medical condition on request and to choose*

their own General Practitioner and Dentist
13) *be consulted on all aspects of living in the Home and nursing care, and have the right to say, 'No'*
14) *go to bed at the chosen time and to have a lie-in as they choose*
15) *have access to the Head of Home, Chief Executive and Inspectorate; have complaints taken seriously and dealt with promptly and fully*

(Reproduced with kind permission of Sister Ann Morrison, General Manager, Crookfur Cottage Homes, Glasgow.)

Collaborative work, including teamwork and a multi-disciplinary approach

Collaborative work is about everyone working together to further the philosophy, aims and objectives of the organisation. It is fully dealt with in Chapter 9 which should be read in conjunction with this section. At this point I merely point out some of the dangers if collaboration and teamwork are absent. If they do not exist it is unlikely that the aims and objectives of an agency can be fully implemented. There is a strong possibility here that collusion among different factions in the care setting will work against a positive care environment, with conflicting groups and cultures arising and separating, for example staff from service users, one group of service users from another or one group of staff from another. As an instance of this, workers on one shift in an agency can incorporate into their culture and value system criticism and antagonism towards staff on another shift. This can become an almost automatic reaction over a period of time, regardless of who the workers are and what they are trying to do. This splits the organisation and in the long run works to the disadvantage rather than the advantage of service users. There can then arise a situation where users collude with staff on one shift to down grade the effectiveness of staff on another shift.

When I mentioned this to a group of students at the end of their first term on placement many of them knew exactly what I was talking about because they had experienced it at first hand. They told me how service users would sometimes exploit different members of staff, knowing that if they did not get something from day shift staff they could probably get what they wanted from the night shift because staff on one shift were already antagonistic to staff on another. This meant that care plans were thwarted by staff working against one another and in the end it was the service user who suffered from a lack of consistency and implementation of the plan of care. Such situations can be dealt a death blow before they even become established if there is effective teamwork with staff communicating with one another, meeting together and being united in their aims and objectives.

There is a wonderful Video Arts film called *Where there's a will*, which demonstrates the ways in which teamwork can either be discouraged or encouraged. Although it is not about a care setting the messages can be applied to any care environment. I have adapted some of these messages to the care environment to illustrate some of the things which are done, often unwittingly, to work against effective teamwork.

- Unit manager to area manager: 'I'm very sorry that Jim's placement with us wasn't successful. It's the poor quality of staff I

have to deal with these days.' This runs down the team.

- Senior care worker to care worker in front of other staff and clients: 'What on earth do you think you're doing? *That's* not the way to do it. Do it like *this*.' This is victimisation and is likely to promote resentment rather than teamwork.

- Unit manager to care worker: 'You shouldn't come asking questions about things which don't concern you. When decisions have been made about who is to be moved to the new unit I'll let you know.' This leaves staff out on a limb and uninvolved in decision making.

- Senior care worker to care worker: 'Why can't you take a leaf out of George's book? He just gets on with the job, head down, doesn't make trouble. He's a very good worker.' This shows favouritism.

Exercise 1

Suggest ways in which the above situations could be used to promote teamwork instead of to discourage it.

Constructive use of time

In one home I visited recently each member of staff was given three activity tasks each day to achieve, for example talking to service users who seemed withdrawn, taking a walk, giving a facial, helping with a craft activity or in the tea room etc., over and above practical tasks such as assisting with bathing and bed making. This ensured that when there were spaces in the day they were used constructively and were not wasted.

Constructive use of time for both service users and staff requires communication, teamwork, thought and planning: communication to find out what people like to do; teamwork in order that staff understand what other staff members are doing; thought to make suggestions; and planning to ensure that activities are carried out in the best possible way.

Effective management

Teamwork and optimising care are maximised if there is management in place which can lead in a democratic, non-authoritarian way. There are some wonderful quotes about this which seem to be born out in practice:

Lead the people, walk behind them.

As for the best leaders, the people do not notice their existence. The next best, the people honour and praise. The next, the people fear; and the next the people hate . . .

When the best leader's work is done the people say, 'We did it ourselves!'

(From Lao-tzu.)

The real leader has no need to lead – he is content to point the way.

(Henry Miller, 1941, The Wisdom of the Heart.)

Ah well! I am their leader, I really ought to follow them!

(Alexandre Auguste Ledru-Rollin (1807–1874).)

Leadership does not depend on being right.

Ivan Illich, American philosopher, New York Review of Books, 1971.

A very good book, *Management Skills in Social Care*, by John Harris and Des Kelly, 1991, covers this subject extremely well and I cannot hope to do it justice here. Since this is not really a book about management I will only touch upon it and refer the reader to the above work for greater inspiration.

Where there is poor management a unit often virtually falls to pieces; I have seen units which have been well run become chaotic in a matter of weeks when a new manager has come onto the scene who does not seem to know what he or she is doing, lacks confidence, seems overwhelmed by the task in hand, gets panic attacks in the most minor crisis, and then blames the situation on others. From the literature about management and from my own experience, mostly at the receiving end, there do seem to be a few things which stand out about what makes an effective manager:

- a willingness to get to know staff strengths and weaknesses, building upon staff strengths and introducing training to counter some of the weaknesses

- a willingness to engage staff in the running of the unit while at the same time establishing authority to make decisions when necessary, though decisions should whenever possible be team decisions

- a commitment to the agency

- relevant experience which enhances understanding of the jobs which social care workers do

- an ability to stay calm and unflustered.

One form of management which I find particularly appealing is management by walking about. This involves being seen around the social care agency at frequent intervals and not sitting closeted in an office. If nothing else this increases the accessibility of the manager and reminds both service users and staff that the manager is interested and involved in what is going on. It ensures that the manager is quickly aware if things are going wrong and is more likely to be included rather than excluded from discussions which take place.

Hemingway (1987) has stressed several important features of management and the leadership which this involves. He stresses the importance of giving people confidence in the value of their job so that they feel that what they are doing is worthwhile, giving people confidence in their value as individuals and giving people confidence in their value as a team so that they do not feel that they are working in isolation.

Supervision

Supervision is very often overlooked; managers make the excuse that there is not enough time for it. There must be time for it. Even when units are understaffed and overworked, supervision is a vital component of care. It serves many purposes: it is an opportunity for staff to discuss their work and areas which are worrying them; it can be used as a training opportunity; and it can be used to give praise which is often lacking in the day to day work of caring. The Social Care Association (1994) has set out other points about supervision, among which are the following:

- it develops an awareness of the worker's roles and responsibilities

- it can be used to clarify the aims of the workplace

- it can encourage motivation where this may be lacking

- it is an opportunity to review and plan work

- it can encourage a service user centred service.

This subject is further developed in the final chapter.

Staff ratios

The fewer staff there are to care for each service user, the greater, in general, are the dangers of institutionalisation. Staff ratios for some forms of care are laid down statutorily, but these are minimum standards. One worker with whom I was discussing this felt that in the home in which she worked, where the staff ratio was one member of staff to six users (all of whom have dementia), there was little opportunity for doing activities whereas when it was one to four it was possible to be quite creative about caring, planning activities and actually achieving them. When I mentioned this to a group of care workers they told me that they frequently worked with a ratio of one member of staff to 10 highly dependent people. What do you think are the consequences of this?

Training

Any organisation which does not have training high on the agenda is failing both service users and workers. Training enhances skill through expanding knowledge, encouraging analytical thinking and a problem solving approach, providing supervised practice and emphasising the value base and the service user at the centre.

The care maintenance and therapeutic environment

This section refers to the ways in which the social care worker in his or her direct work with service users can utilise or take advantage of the care setting to provide a life which is as fulfilling as possible, to maintain the service user as a member of society and develop his or her potential. It includes an examination of the potential which the care setting offers for direct care, maximising independence, developing social skills and working with groups and groupings.

Direct care and organising the events of daily living

The enormous importance of the direct care role of social care is often undervalued, underestimated and certainly under-rewarded. The everyday life of any establishment is enhanced if attention is paid to how the tasks of everyday life are achieved. In addition, it is often these everyday tasks which provide the greatest opportunities for establishing relationships with service users, sharing activities and using their potential for managing difficult behaviour or developing social skills. One care worker I spoke to said that one of her outstanding memories was of helping a child to tie his shoe laces on his first day at school. It was so important to him that someone cared about how he looked and realised how important this day was to him. The help was as symbolic as it was practical. It set the seal on an on-going and productive helping relationship.

The establishment of a daily routine which incorporates specific tasks which have to be achieved can also be of great importance to some service users. This can provide structure to previously unstructured lives and enhance skills in daily living (shopping, washing up, cleaning etc.). Where these skills are lacking they can be modelled by the social care worker and practised by the service user. The care setting provides the ideal opportunity for this within an environment which is comfortable for the user and with someone with whom he or she has a close and trusting relationship.

Getting up, meal times and bed time

The importance of these crucial times in everyone's lives are also often underscored in social care settings. The way in which they are tackled can make the difference between people feeling good about their lives or absolutely dreadful. Staff who see having to assist people to get up in the morning as a chore, cannot be cheerful about it, do not make an effort to converse or make this a pleasant time, set the tone for a bad day.

Meal times too are so often opportunities lost. Staff may scuttle off to the staff room leaving one overworked soul to 'supervise' proceedings. Why not all sit down together, at least sometimes? There can be conversation, a mutual getting to know one another, a modelling of behaviour by staff. Service users can be invited to share in the preparation of meals where this is possible; special regard should be given to people's likes, dislikes and cultural needs. When the two Spanish gentlemen referred to in Chapter 5 were admitted to a residential home one of the care staff was heard to say, 'And I expect the next thing will be we'll be expected to make special meals for them.' Well, what can you say to that? Meals *are* important and should be treated as such. They should be discussed, they can be the occasion for giving treats, showing love and care and developing social and practical skills.

In one children's home, the takeaway on Fridays was a major event. There was discussion about what kind of takeaway, how much could be afforded, the outing to go to fetch it and the disappointment to be coped with if the month's budget did not allow for very much. Tea and scones at the local small café was established by one social care student on placement in a home for elderly people. One member of the care staff asked why she was going to all this trouble. She could bring scones in on her way to work and it would be so much easier to have them in the home, just the way they always had. This did rather miss the point. How?

Bed time – that time to be looked forward to at the end of the day. You might like to use it to wind down, curl up with the lamp on, in a nice bed with a cup of hot chocolate and/or someone you love. How do service users in your agency like bed time? Do you know? Is this what they get? Or is it a time when staff absolutely cannot wait to get off duty or have a break and some peace and quiet? Is bed time dealt with peacefully at a leisurely pace and has the significance of it ever been thought about?

If you are involved in bed time, what is the best way of going about it? Do any changes need to be made? Is there any choice for adults? Is there agreement among staff in a children's home about how to deal with those who will not go to bed or who get up again if they do? A planned behavioural approach may be appropriate here or just a change in staff

attitudes. Just being nice and pleasant, relaxed and calm, willing to provide a hot drink, willing to read a story to tired children or chat about the events of the day with any service user may prevent problems from developing and considerably ease those which already exist. This is therapeutic intervention. It does not have to have a fancy name. It does sound a bit idealistic given staff shortages and unplanned crises, but without ideals there can be no progress.

Activities and holidays

Although activities have already been referred to in discussing working with groups in the previous section, I refer to them again here as particularly important and useful in work in any care environment. Doing an activity together is a splendid way of getting to know the service user group, for them to get to know you, of adding interest, challenge, development of skill and enjoyment to the lives of those with whom we work. It can also be very therapeutic, in the sense that it helps to relieve stress, raise self esteem and have spin-offs in other areas of life. When I worked in a day centre for elderly people in New York State, one of the activities in which I was involved was an illustration group: no talent or previous experience needed. The pictures we all produced were important to everyone – creating something usually is – but there were other things just as important, though perhaps not consciously acknowledged: company, conversation, the time out and timelessness of the activity, the chance it gave to relax completely and the fact that we all agreed that it did not matter if our works were not masterpieces, it was the doing of them which mattered. When some of them were masterpieces this was an added bonus. I remember particularly the bird's nest, drawn by one man who had Parkinson's disease. He managed a degree of control over his movement which was quite miraculous, in view of his lack of control at other times, and week after week he meticulously reproduced each tiny blade of grass and twig and oddment which had gone into the making of the bird's nest. We all appreciated birds' nests by the end of that exercise.

Obviously holidays do not take place *in* the service user's usual setting but the setting can be the location from which they are organised, and it is the users of the setting who will benefit from them. Holidays in lovely places have lots of spin-offs apart from being, in general, thoroughly enjoyable experiences. They can be an occasion for:

• enabling service users to choose where to go and what they want to do

• planning

• gaining new experiences

• sharing

• feeling free from the constraints of everyday life

• staff and service users to get to know one another in a relaxed and friendly way

• sharing memories after the event, which gives a sense of bonding to those who participated

I recently arrived at a school for children with learning difficulties on the first day back after the annual trip to the Lake District. I sat with the senior class of 12-year-olds and older who had quite severe learning difficulties and enjoyed looking at the photographs with them. I had already got to know them over the course of the past year and there was much pleasure and laughter as we looked at George abseiling in his wheelchair, Susan and Jo underground in a cave, John wandering off over a field as was his habit, the whole group enjoying a meal in the chalet, everyone on the bus on the way there and back and the trip in the pony and trap. All of this would enrich their experience of school for the whole of the year to come; they had been with their teachers and social care workers in a different setting and they could all laugh together in a way which had been impossible before. They had also gained so much in confidence, self esteem, relationships with one another and new skills. Doors had been opened which, before the holiday, would have seemed eternally closed.

Meetings

Meetings of or with service users can take many forms, ranging from meetings of or with the whole service user group, to meetings with small groups of representatives. Whatever their composition they can provide an opportunity for all of those present to air views and feel that they have a stake in the way things are run. They are a further way of establishing and practising the principles of social care: of enhancing the dignity of individuals, enabling them to express choices and stand up for their rights and of acknowledging different cultures and planning for these. Meetings present an opportunity to let off steam before explosion levels are reached and for service users and staff to be in touch with one another's feelings and perspectives. They are also a means of readjusting power structures and empowering service users through enabling them to participate in the decision making process.

Exercise 2

In examining your own establishment, how are meetings used? Could their use be improved upon?

Incorporating other methods of implementing plans

The other approaches discussed – task-centred work, behavioural work, the use of networks, counselling and group work – all lend themselves to being implemented within a care environment by social carers, even though other professionals such as qualified social workers, psychologists and medical practitioners may also be involved. If several people are working with a service user, possibly from different disciplines, it is essential that they work together, rather than in separate compartments. It is so easy for staff to be by-passed unless they can articulate their work to these others in the multi-disciplinary team and demonstrate their skill, understanding and value base. The value of 'the other 23 hours' can be overlooked by other professionals who come in for an hour or two (or less) for a therapeutic purpose and then attribute all of the progress to themselves . . . unless the social care workers themselves can demonstrate their value and participate fully in the assessment, planning, implementation and evaluation process.

Social care workers have many advantages over others involved in the care

of the service user. They very often are with him or her for more hours of the day and night than anyone else, they get to know all of his or her moods and phases and can implement plans along with the tasks of everyday life. All of this gives social care workers a unique advantage for helping in the context of the care environment. This has given rise to theoretical approaches which incorporate aspects of those approaches already discussed into a blend specially adapted to social care settings. Such ideas were developed by Redl and Wineman in the USA, and by way of concluding this section I present a few ideas which they present about the 'life space' of the care setting together with a few concluding ideas derived from other sections of this book.

Social care settings can:

1) Be places where people can be helped, in a secure and caring environment, to face the consequences of their actions.

2) Support people in maximising what they can do, leading to a healthier sense of self and raising self esteem.

3) Offer opportunities for modelling behaviour by staff, for establishing and demonstrating values. This is illustrated through the use of that part of the behavioural approach entitled models in Chapter 7.

4) Offer the opportunity to learn or improve upon life skills, including day to day behaviour. The second strand of behavioural work is particularly relevant here.

5) Maximise opportunities for choice,

empowerment and autonomy as a means of nurturing and enhancing a sense of self and raising self esteem.

6) Provide a setting for working with groups and groupings.

7) Provide a safe and sensitive environment which can play a part in diminishing challenging behaviour or in which challenging behaviour can be confronted and dealt with. Here such methods as behavioural work, gentle teaching and therapeutic crisis intervention can be used (see Chapter 7).

Community environment

Promoting links with families and the wider community

Since they are closely integrated into all of the aspects of the care environment approach, the importance of family/friendship ties and links with the wider community should be emphasised. There will be service users who may need protection from some of these links or a great deal of support in maintaining them, and there are links with the wider community which could be seen as intrusive and invasive. This whole issue, then, should be approached with care and thought and it should not be assumed that the promotion of all such links is necessarily a good thing. However, there is a great deal of evidence which suggests that social care environments which fail to promote links with family and community networks can become isolated, institutionalised and are more likely to give rise to settings in which service users are neglected or abused. Elkan and Kelly

(1991) discuss some of this evidence. They mention the Barclay Report which emphasises the importance, in residential settings, of maintaining family and community links, and an unpublished work by Clough (1987) into scandals in residential centres, which was presented as evidence to the Wagner Committee. Clough was particularly concerned about abuses of power and generally poor practice in settings which received few outside visitors. Some of the positive benefits of family and community links are illustrated in discussions of service user networks in Chapter 7. The value of community links is also discussed in Chapter 4.

As a conclusion I mention recent emphasis upon seeing social care settings as part of the community and as community resources. One building, previously only used as an adult training centre, now also houses a community nursery, a drop-in coffee shop and crèche, and a welfare benefits adviser. It has developed links with the local community college which students attend and which also uses the centre for some outreach courses, including an English course for people for whom English is not their first language. Students of the adult training centre often gain work placements in the nursery, and boundaries among the various services have become very flexible. The development of resource centres seems to be one way forward in breaking down barriers, though such provision must be carefully planned to take account of all service user needs.

Exercise 3

Think about the advantages and disadvantages for someone in a residential home if that home also provides a range of services for the local community. How do you think some of these difficulties may be overcome?

Suggestions for further reading

- Ainsworth, F. and Fulcher, L. (eds.) (1981) *Group Care for Children*. London: Tavistock.

A classic which still holds true for work with children in care.

- Davis, L. (1992) *Social Care, Rivers of Pain, Bridges of Hope*. London: Whiting and Birch.

An interesting and varied collection of Davis' writing over a number of years about caring, feelings, management, stress and many other things; the book also provides an international perspective. There are lots of literary quotes, and it is an enjoyable as well as an enlightening read.

- Ward, A. (1993) *Working in Group Care*. Birmingham: Venture Press.

This is an excellent book which looks at work in group care, the service user's stay and the worker's shift.

Collaborative work

. . . it became clear that collaboration with service users and carers, and collaboration between different groups of practitioners, should not be treated separately but as a unified concept of community care.

BERESFORD AND TREILLION, 1995.

. . . team work should never be regarded as an optional extra in this sort of work: it is the heart of the matter.

WARD, 1993.

Collaborative work involves crossing the boundaries of personal and agency function to share planning, action and joint responsibility for the outcome of practice. It is all about working together to produce the best possible results. It is a holistic approach to care which looks at the big picture and is not confined by disciplinary boundaries or defensive practice. Community care requires, more than ever before, that service users, workers, agencies and those of different disciplines work together, i.e. collaborate, to provide an optimum service. This is all very fine as a statement, but is this what happens in practice? What is needed to make this a reality?

Some of the factors needed can come from individual workers, some from management and some from the way in which services are organised. The emphasis in this chapter is on the skills which you as individual workers can use to promote collaboration, although there are also outside factors to consider such as management and agency structures. The first section focuses on collaboration in a

very general way, looking at the skills which are needed to put it into effect. This is followed by sections on different kinds of collaboration: collaboration in the workplace (teamwork and co-working) and collaboration outside the workplace (working with outside agencies, with communities and multi-disciplinary work). Figure 9.1 on p. 114 illustrates this.

Skills of collaborative work
Communication and relationships

Formal and informal, verbal, including written, non-verbal and symbolic communication, are all important in collaborative work. It is especially important to avoid meaningless jargon, to listen attentively, observe carefully and to communicate thoughtfully. A willingness to work at relationships with service users, colleagues and all others involved in care is fundamental to collaborative work. Working on relationships is not enough. The social care worker also needs to understand these relationships in terms of the influences of discrimination and power

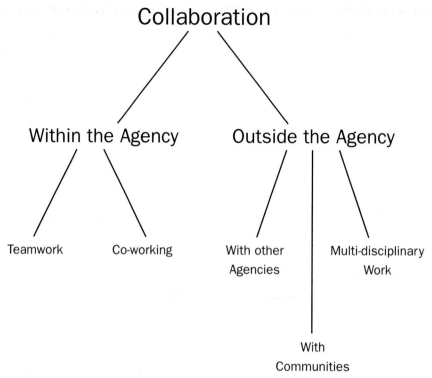

Figure 9.1: Collaboration

differences while countering the inappropriate features of these influences in so far as this is possible. Often, both the social care worker and the service user are placed in situations where others discriminate or misuse their power, thus preventing optimum care. The social care worker needs the ability to recognise these situations and where appropriate to advocate on the service user's behalf or on his or her own behalf.

Flexibility

To work well collaboratively the individual requires adaptability, open-mindedness and a willingness to learn from the skills of others, all of which comprise flexibility.

Negotiation

This is a need and willingness to discuss

issues, consult service users, colleagues and management. Sometimes it involves compromise or confrontation in finding optimum solutions to care.

Partnership

This means working with others and needs a willingness and ability to work alongside all relevant others, especially service users and colleagues, sharing ideas, work practices and information without feeling threatened by them encroaching upon 'your' work or invading 'your' territory, and working together for the good of the service user without being territorial or possessive. This involves all of the preceding skills of communication, flexibility and negotiation.

Evaluation

Collaborative work must be accompanied by some form of evaluation. This is the ability to reflect upon all aspects of the collaborative process in order to evaluate whether it is being used to maximum effect. It means assessing whether what is happening is as good as it can be. Evaluation will also point the way to developing future collaborative work in terms of the next steps to be taken and who is responsible for which aspects of the work.

Recognising the limitations

Sometimes perfection just is not possible. You may be able to see the ideal but within the limitations of your role, time constraints or the people you are working with the attainment of perfection is impossible. Sometimes you have to learn to live with the less than perfect but the best you can do given the circumstances, be happy with it and not bitter or resentful or dispirited. This too is a skill. It is about getting on with the job without letting negative feelings of disappointment get in the way. It does not mean throwing ideals out of the window – they can still be fought for – but it does mean that on a day to day basis you have to collaborate as well as possible given the circumstances you have.

Exercise 1

How do you think collaborative work could help the student who wrote the following comment?:

Unfortunately I am unable to challenge workmates in this situation as they have mocked me in the past

when I did challenge a member of staff who made racist comments. I am aware of how important this issue is and realise that I should try to do something about it, although at the same time I am concerned as it could make the situation worse, as there are very few people who share the same values.

In looking at this exercise you may have considered:

1) **Communication** – if there had been clear communication of the values and principles of care to all workers it is likely that many of the workers would be challenging racist comments. If there were lines of communication for staff to state their views in a non-threatening, secure situation such as supervision or a team meeting, the worker could have felt supported and able to share his concerns.

2) **Flexibility** – if other staff members had been flexible it would have meant that they were open-minded, willing to learn, willing to listen to a different point of view, willing to change if change was in the best interests of service users.

3) **Negotiation** – if negotiation skills were being practised within the workplace, workers would be willing to discuss issues and compromise if it was in the cause of improving quality of life for service users.

4) **Partnership** – if staff had been working together for the benefit of

service users against a background of a social care value base, there would have been no question of prejudice or a member of staff making racist comments without being challenged.

After reading the section on teamwork you may wish to add further comments about how this form of collaboration could enhance the worker's ability to challenge racism and work for optimum quality of life for service users. Susan Gibb makes reference to this element of social care practice in Chapter 3.

Teamwork

Teamwork is viewed here as that part of collaborative work which takes place within an agency, whether it is a residential, day care or other community setting. The team is a vital ingredient of good social care practice and consists of a group of people who work together to achieve the philosophy and goals of their agency. It is evident from this definition that a group of people working together does not necessarily constitute a team. The team concept presupposes that there are common goals which everyone should be working together towards achieving. This takes careful thought and organisation and requires all of the qualities of collaborative work already discussed: communication, relationships, flexibility, negotiation, working in partnership with others and evaluation. Teamwork also requires commitment to the ideal of a team and to the team's goals.

The prerequisites of teamwork can be encouraged by good leadership, showing team members that their work and their views are valued and emphasising that only through everyone working together

can the aims of the team be achieved. Good teamwork requires people to feel like a team, to think like a team and to act like a team. Ways in which this can be achieved are:

- through team meetings, across shifts if this is appropriate and possible, to enable those who would not normally communicate to do so

- involving service users in meetings whenever possible

- enabling informal communication through accessibility of management to staff and service users

- ensuring that decisions made at team meetings are put into action

- using praise and encouragement where this is due

- utilising staff strengths and encouraging individuality

- promoting a team philosophy.

A great deal of social care practice can *only* be done effectively as a team for several reasons:

1) Several workers may be working with the same person and need to co-ordinate their efforts.

2) In group care settings such as day centres and residential homes the only effective way to work is as a team with everyone working towards the same goals. If there are people who are ignoring the team principle and developing their own way of working

independently and without reference to other team members, there arises 'private practice' which might look like a good idea at the time but is usually detrimental in the long term to the team effort.

Exercise 2

Write down or discuss with others the possible detrimental effects of independent 'private practice'.

This does not negate the importance of workers taking the initiative, but stresses the point that if they do and they have ideas which they would like to put into effect then for optimum outcome they should be part of a team effort or at least discussed at team level. However, if there is no team then individual initiative might be the only way to promote change and may in itself be conducive to promoting discussion at team level.

Here are some points which you may have thought of in response to the above exercise. You may well have thought of others. Some possible detrimental effects of private practice are:

- other workers may resent it

- it may be counter to other efforts

- if it is planned independently it cannot be integrated into the work of the agency

- the individual worker is unlikely to get help from other workers

- it may mean that a care plan is not fully

implemented or is implemented in different ways by different workers

Much social care practice is visible practice, done in front of other workers and service users, and the way in which it is done affects many people. If there is no general agreement among staff, and conflicts and difficulties go unresolved because of the lack of team functioning, this is felt and noticed by service users and can affect their well-being, their sense of belonging and the ability of workers and users to achieve the goals which they have set for themselves.

Team meetings

Here one of the essential ingredients of teamwork is considered in greater detail: the team meeting.

Who should attend?

One of the first questions to be raised is 'who comes to team meetings?' This necessitates examination of who are the members of the team:

1) Does the team consist only of those who are employed to work directly with service users or should it also include domestic, administrative and other staff?

2) What about service users? Should they or their representative attend team meetings?

These are questions which have to be answered by each individual agency and according to the kind of meeting being held, but at least the questions should be raised and an assumption should not be made that only 'direct' workers should be involved. Often, domestic staff communicate a great deal with service users and have knowledge and influence which care staff do not have; sometimes users choose to communicate with administrative staff. In the day centre in which I worked all staff attended team meetings and were equally regarded: full-time staff, part-time staff, kitchen staff, volunteer organisers, social care workers, instructors, administrative staff and managers. The team meeting itself was an opportunity to share ideas, raise concerns, share information, and a means of consolidating team spirit and discussing areas of difficulty and conflict. It was an avenue for the discussion of such issues as discrimination and for making specific resolutions about anti-discriminatory practice. Nationality, colour, gender, disability, culture and religion are often matters which are avoided rather than discussed. The team meeting should be safe enough for such issues to be raised and talked about openly both in terms of staff and service users. The team leader plays a pivotal role in enabling this process to take place.

Team meetings may take several forms. There are some meetings which only a small group of relevant workers needs to attend and where it would be disadvantageous to have too many people present: review discussions about a particular service user, for example, or discussion about some issues of staff discipline which involve particular workers, but for discussion of matters which affect the whole team then the whole team should have the opportunity to attend.

Successful team meetings

There are several prerequisites if team meetings are to succeed. Among these are:

1) **Appropriate participation of members** – it is no good having team meetings if members are not willing or permitted to participate.

2) **Dissemination of information** – whenever possible members should receive information relevant to their functioning as full team members. This may be in the form of minutes of the previous meeting, an agenda to which they have had an opportunity to contribute and information received by the agency which is relevant to their work.

3) **Consideration of timing** – in agencies where there are night staff and staff on several different shifts and/or different geographically separate units, major problems arise if all members do not meet or communicate in any way. They can develop their own cultures and ways of doing things, or have a separate agenda which detracts from optimising the quality of life for service users. Some agencies overcome this by timing meetings at shift change-over times or by paying staff to come in for meetings at times when they would not normally be working. Some agencies integrate the work of different shifts through a mixture of daily hand-over meetings, occasional all-staff meetings and supervision of individual staff. Other agencies ignore the issue altogether to their peril. The result can be a lack of integrated work, one staff group against another, the development of a false picture about

staff on one shift as opposed to another and service users playing off one group of staff against another. The possibilities for less than optimal care in such a situation are many.

4) **Location of meeting** – if possible, this should be away from the day to day running of the agency in a comfortable place.

5) **Advance preparation** – this should be by both the team leader (if there is one) and team members. Members may rotate responsibility for preparing meetings where this is appropriate, in order that organisation is not always seen as the province of one person.

6) **Structure to the meeting** – meetings, if they are not to disintegrate into a meaningless ramble, should have a structure which is more or less adhered to. Structures can have some flexibility but without a structure it is not likely that much will be achieved.

7) **Constructive use of time** – two of the criticisms often levelled at meetings is that they are either a waste of time or that they take up too much time. If the meeting is well planned and structured, is seen to be relevant and is time limited and focused it is much more likely to achieve positive results.

A really frustrating meeting would look a bit like this:

• no information at all beforehand except that there is going to be a team meeting

• the person who called the meeting in the first place is very late and keeps everyone waiting

• there is no refreshment and this is a break time

• the meeting is held in the main office and the telephone keeps ringing

• there are some new faces but no-one is formally introduced

• the meeting is totally dominated by the concerns of the 'team leader'

• the whole atmosphere is rushed

• no-one is properly listened to and everyone comes away feeling thoroughly disgruntled and demoralised

So much for team spirit.

A well planned team meeting may be like this:

• a time, place, previous minutes and a request for proposals for the agenda are circulated a week beforehand (a week! well, at least beforehand)

• there is coffee or tea and a relaxed atmosphere on the day of the meeting

• the usual interruptions (especially telephones) are minimised

• the meeting starts on time

• everyone is welcomed

• new members are introduced to everyone else

• the meeting is structured according to the agenda

• everyone is enabled to feel that his or

her voice is relevant and that he or she is listened to

- the chairperson of the meeting ensures that no one person (including him or herself) dominates the meeting and/or makes others feel that they do not have a relevant part to play

- all matters are covered

- issues which require longer discussion are either held over to the next meeting or allocated special time

- the meeting finishes on time

In social care there will be circumstances beyond anyone's control which mean that sometimes meetings are less than perfect. For example, a crisis occurs which must be dealt with before the meeting can begin, a crucial member is off sick, the previous minutes are not typed because of excessive demands upon administrative staff, the meeting comes after several very demanding days and everyone is feeling rather tired and stressed. But these should not be used as excuses for not striving for the ideal.

Further general prescriptions would be ridiculous. Each agency has its own functions, way of working, membership and leadership, and to set out any further prescription for the ideal team meeting would be neither profitable nor realistic. But the importance of the team and team meetings needs repeated emphasis because working in social care is essentially working as a member of a team in the interests of the service user.

Advantages of teamwork

As a conclusion to this section I have set out what seem to be the main advantages of teamwork. The team:

- is greater than the sum of its parts; it can make things happen which could not happen if the team did not exist

- can provide help and support to members

- can co-ordinate the activities of individuals

- can identify training and development needs

- can provide a satisfying, stimulating and enjoyable working environment

- can co-ordinate areas of expertise so that those with different skills can join forces to enhance individual practice

- provides learning opportunities through participation and discussion of issues

- can help to provide a more comprehensive service to service users

- enables workers to look at problems in the context of the whole situation and to look at how parts fit together as a whole

Co-working

Co-working occurs when two or more workers collaborate to work with a service user or a group by working directly with them either at the same time or by agreement at different times towards agreed goals. Ideas about co-working have been mainly developed in relation to co-keyworking, where workers share the task of keyworker to a client, and in relation to group work, where workers share the organisation and/or running of a group. It can also apply to the everyday tasks of social care.

One care worker had responsibility for the bar evening and setting up activities at the home in which she worked. She felt that this would be a job better done by two people and asked if one of the new social care workers could carry this out with her. This had several advantages: the two workers could pool ideas and tasks; the new worker, who was somewhat lacking in confidence, could build this up and gain in self esteem and motivation through taking responsibility; it made the whole job of organisation less of a chore and much more enjoyable; and co-working in one situation facilitated working together in others.

Co-keyworking

In relation to keyworking there are both advantages and disadvantages to co-keyworking and the former must clearly outweigh the latter if it is to be a success. Mallinson (1995), in his research into co-keyworking, found that it was practised in 47% of establishments with keyworker systems. He identifies four different kinds of co-keyworking:

1) Based on hierarchy – for example where there are junior and senior staff working together.

2) Based on teams – for example in small units where keyworkers work together.

3) Based on formal pairing – for example when staff on different shifts act across for each other.

4) Based on pragmatic arrangements – for example to cover periods of holiday or sickness or when more demanding or disabled service users need two workers.

Co-keyworking, when it is working well, can have many advantages for the service user, as follows:

• Two different perspectives are gained, which widens choice and gives the service user two different people to talk to and discuss things with. No one worker is likely to dominate the situation and the service user is protected from exploitation by one worker.

• The wishes of the service user, for example for a female keyworker or a black keyworker, can be partly overcome if there is co-keyworking since workers in short supply can be allocated to twice as many people.

• There can be more sharing among staff of both their different skills and characteristics.

• Co-keyworkers can cover for absences, so that absences become less demoralising for the service user. Also, the possibility of 24-hour keycover becomes more of a reality and there is more likelihood of someone from an outside agency being able to speak to a keyworker.

• If a keyworker leaves there can still be continuity of care. A new keyworker can pair up with an existing keyworker.

• Co-keyworking promotes

communication and teamwork and keyworkers are less likely to feel isolated. They can offer one another mutual support and can share their areas of expertise.

Where there is a philosophy of collaboration and teamwork, co-keyworking is more likely to be a success. Dangers arise where this is not the case, for example if two co-keyworkers compete against each other or collude with one another to the exclusion of the service user. What do you envisage as the consequences of this? The task becomes very difficult indeed when two workers do not get on with one another, where one works much harder than the other (or thinks he or she does) or where workers do not share the same values and ideas. So at the heart of good, successful co-keyworking there are the constant necessities of good communication, good relationships, good leadership and good teamwork.

Group work

These are also prerequisites for co-working in group work, which can consist of co-leading, co-planning, co-evaluating and/or co-running a group. The co-workers will need to agree beforehand about who is doing what. Within the group they may perform different, agreed roles. For example, one leader will concentrate on the task or exercise which is planned while the other tries to draw in reluctant participants or deals with control issues. There are two important considerations here:

1) It is important that the co-workers swap roles sometimes so that one is not labelled 'the leader' or 'the soft touch' (or something else).

2) The co-workers should agree not to undermine one another by taking over their agreed roles.

Collaboration outside the agency

No one agency can expect to provide for all of the needs of all service users unless it is a total institution ... and the disadvantages of a total institution have already been outlined (see Chapter 1). Links with other agencies are vital and should be carefully nurtured. These links, as with all other collaborative work, require good communication, good relationships and good recording of information. 'Good' here refers to developed to as high a standard as possible. It requires effort (the Oomph factor) – effort to make the communications in the first place and to make them with preparation in advance, effort to keep the links going even in the face of difficulties and a sometimes negative or unenthusiastic response, and a willingness to keep a record of communications which may be useful in present and future work.

The host organisation

The first level of collaboration with an outside agency is with the 'host' organisation, if there is one. For instance, the 'host' organisation for a local authority children's home is usually the social services or social work department. This requires links with the local district office as well as headquarters. It is important for social care workers to have knowledge of how the host organisation works as a whole. It is usually this organisation which determines overall policy, sanctions work done and provides a protective umbrella. Of course, the communication and collaboration have to be in both directions, to and from the agency and to and from the host organisation; the extent of the communication determines the amount and nature of the collaboration which can take place. If there is a very rigid, formal hierarchy, and a democratic, participatory and consultative approach is not encouraged, then it is very difficult for an agency to feel that it is in partnership with the host organisation. Although this may seem to present insurmountable difficulties it is, in such a situation, necessary for the agency to make its views known. Where consultative, constructive meetings are lacking, views can always be expressed in writing. The attempt and the effort matter. The organisation will not always communicate with participating agencies and it is sometimes not that headquarters is purposely ignoring the contribution which agencies can make but it has neglected to realise the value of their contribution.

Relationships with other agencies under the same host umbrella are also important. These agencies should collaborate, complement and supplement one another while working for the good of the whole. In such a situation being in competition is not usually constructive.

Other agencies

Collaboration and involvement with other agencies will to a large extent be determined by their purpose, their catchment area and the relationship which

is built up with them. One worker in a voluntary organisation residential school told me that his agency collaborated with the following: social services; psychological services; education departments; intermediate treatment groups; the police; health centres; hospitals; other children's homes and residential schools; supported accommodation agencies; and sport and leisure facilities. Community police are becoming increasingly willing to collaborate with children's services, and often visit children's homes and residential schools in a effort to promote positive links. Collaboration is not just promoted through formal meetings and reviews but also through telephone contact, written communication and informal social occasions. Good collaboration among agencies unites them in implementing care plans effectively.

The local community

As community care develops so caring agencies should be seen increasingly as part of the community, in the community for the community. This has for a long time been the case in many instances and is not just the result of the 1990 legislation. Most residential and day care establishments have probably maintained and nurtured more community links than most households in their areas (though probably not as many as the potential number of households represented by service users) and far from being isolated, have often worked hard to foster good relationships with their neighbourhood. The core and cluster project described in Chapter 4 is one in which relationships were worked at very hard. At first neighbours were suspicious; they were very interested in what was going on but wary and unwilling to make any initial approach to workers or users of the project. Project workers tackled this by:

1) Attending a meeting of the local residents association and explaining the project to them.

2) Inviting representatives of the association to come to see one of the flats and taking this opportunity to enable members to put themselves in the shoes of the service users.

3) Not getting angry when local residents appeared prejudiced against the project, but gently explaining its nature and purpose; showing understanding of why local residents may feel some resentment but also showing that the resentment was ill founded because it was a local project serving the needs of local people.

4) Not confining day care at the project to service users in residence but opening it to referrals, including self-referrals, from the local neighbourhood.

5) Providing recreational activities to local residents who were assessed as being in need of them. For example, project workers have been assisting local residents to the pub and on shopping trips.

By taking 'day care' to the people some important lessons have been learned: a 'centre' is not always necessary and need may be more appropriately met by assisting people to use 'normal' community facilities rather than creating a service in a special building. Although small groups of people can be catered for in this way, when larger numbers of people require a service a day care facility does have advantages of requiring fewer members of staff to provide for the needs of more people. Perhaps a combination of the two approaches, with the judicious use of volunteers, can overcome problems associated with the two approaches.

Multi-disciplinary work

Although this is both collaborative and team work it is worth emphasising the value of multi-disciplinary work in its own right, where this is appropriate for the fulfilment of need. It is a prerequisite of maximising the benefit of community care to the service user. Work in some organisations crosses disciplinary boundaries more readily than others. Work in a hospice, for example, is likely to involve the work of people of many different disciplines – nurses, social workers, health and social care workers, doctors, administrative staff, people with skills in complementary medicine and many others – working together with the service user and family in caring together. Figure 9.2 puts the service user and family at the centre of the process, treating the individual as a whole person in a situation rather than as a collection of diagnostic labels. The team, of course, will vary according to the needs of the service user.

In a hostel for people with learning disabilities members of the multi-disciplinary team may include social care workers, managers, training centre instructors, social workers, psychologists, advocates, police personnel, health workers, staff from local hospitals and staff

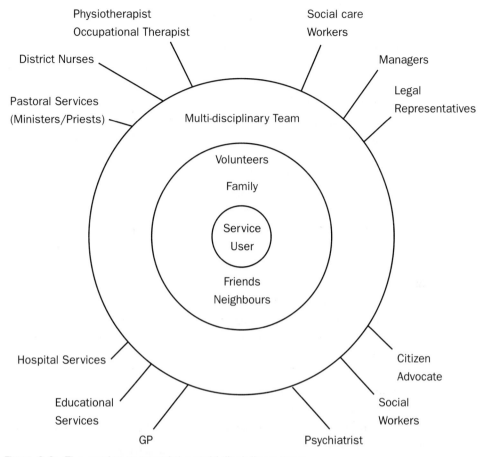

Figure 9.2: The service user and the multi-disciplinary team

of other supported accommodation. They will bring with them different perspectives and knowledge, and through collaboration they can optimise care for the service user.

Problems arise, as in any other form of team work, where some individuals exercise their power independently and forget to consult with other team members in making important decisions. One example of this may be where the careful planning of a multi-disciplinary team, including a keyworker and advocate, has resulted in a young man moving from a large hospital into a small hostel where he has a lot more freedom and independence.

After a minor accident the consultant psychiatrist and the manager of the hostel arrange for the return of the young man to the hospital from which he has been discharged. This sets the whole programme worked on by the team back by several months when the crisis could, in all probability and with a multi-disciplinary team approach, have been coped with within the hostel setting. Re-admission to hospital is seen by the service user as punishment and all work towards empowerment, normalisation and independence goes out of the window.

Multi-disciplinary work especially

requires a willingness to confront others with a different way of looking at a situation as well as a willingness to look at things yourself in new ways. The success of community care depends to a large extent upon this. Boundaries which have divided disciplines, and stereotypes which are carried around of different professional groups, have to succumb to the rationale of a multi-disciplinary approach. Some ways of doing this are to ensure that all appropriate disciplines are represented at reviews and for workers to attend multi-disciplinary discussions and conferences.

One way which I have found useful in promoting a multi-disciplinary approach in a hospice setting is to participate in training sessions together with members of different disciplines such as nurses and doctors. In presenting ourselves as a multi-disciplinary team to an audience we were forced into discussion of our roles and we all gained in understanding of one another. I think a lot of progress in mutual understanding can be made through having to talk as a team to others about what you do, and the hospice movement has been at the forefront of such an approach.

Multi-disciplinary work does not mean that you reduce your own area of expertise and does not diminish in any way the knowledge and skill gained through training and experience in a particular discipline. It demands the same prerequisites as any other form of collaboration, and so the end of this chapter is its beginning. Collaboration, whether it is teamwork, co-keyworking,

working with the local community or multi-disciplinary work, constantly harks back to the importance of communication, negotiation, flexibility, partnership and evaluation.

Exercise 3

Look at an agency in which you work or are on placement or know well and:

- briefly describe the collaborative work which goes on both inside the agency and with the outside world

- identify the factors which affect this collaborative work

- evaluate the effectiveness of
  - teamwork
  - collaboration with outside agencies

Suggestions for further reading

- Novan, A. (1994) *Collaboration in Community Care in the 1990s.* Business Education Publishers.

  Novan provides a very thorough examination of all aspects of collaborative work.

- Ward, A. (1993) *Working in Group Care.* Birmingham: Venture Press.

  This book provides an excellent section on teamwork, with examples.

10 | Writing things down – records and reports

Although at one time seen as a troublesome chore which reduced the time available for client contact, record keeping is beginning to be recognised as a core skill in which, where possible, clients participate.

COULSHED, 1991.

'I haven't got time for that nonsense.' 'I do things, I don't write things.' 'I can't write anyway.' Do any of these sound familiar? Yet records and reports are vital elements of communication and the social care worker's task, an integral part of the caring process. They are part of showing respect for the worth and dignity of the individual and are at the heart of assessment, care planning, implementation and evaluation. Increasingly the emphasis is upon shared, open recording – seeing the record as a useful tool in the helping process. Recording and report writing are not just about someone but with someone.

Writing things down has some distinct advantages. The written word can be deliberated upon, evaluated and in the light of this altered. It can also be kept and referred to by different people from those who wrote it. These could also be seen as disadvantages, as could the following:

• the written word often takes on a life of its own and can become the last word on an issue just because it is written down

• writing as a form of communication does not have the give and take of other forms of communication

• not everyone is good at it so that reports can vary in quality from one worker to another

Some of these disadvantages can be overcome, some of them are in the nature of this form of communication. The written word should never be seen as replacing discussion; it complements discussion and provides a way of recording information which needs to be kept or passed on. One aim of this section is to emphasise that social care workers have a useful and credible part to play in this facet of communication, implementation and collaboration.

Information in records and reports should at least be useful, valid, relevant and have significant purpose. It should be written in a way which is easily understandable to others with attention given to grammar and spelling (a dictionary can be useful), especially where such reports will be passed on to others. There are few things worse than receiving a rambling, opinionated, careless and untidy report – such a report is an insult to the worth, dignity and rights of the service user.

Types of recording and report writing

Recording can take many forms. One major distinction can be made between formal records and informal records. Formal records are those which must be kept about a service user as part of agency policy; informal records are those written in order to improve the service to the service user. Some of the latter may be included in formal agency records, but this is not always the case. They may, for example, just consist of what a worker and service user have written down in order to understand and clarify a situation. The understanding gained may form part of a formal record, but the jottings themselves need not necessarily do so.

Recording is on-going, and can be distinguished from report writing which occurs at particular times for a specified purpose, for example review reports and incident reports. These may draw upon agency records for their content and will be incorporated into a service user's case record. Examples of recording and report writing are:

1) The daily report (really a record of what has occurred on a particular shift) – this is not a substitute for a hand-over meeting but an aid to it and of some use to those who missed the hand-over or who have been away from the workplace for a day or longer.

2) The report book – this may record big issues carried over from the daily report and may be used in distinguishing particular patterns of events and perhaps what led up to them.

3) Incident report – this may be separate from or included in the report book and serves a similar purpose.

4) Service user and worker diaries – a form of recording.

5) Individual case files.

6) Monthly summaries for individual case files.

7) Minutes of meetings.

8) Supervision reports.

9) Review reports.

Whatever form the writing of records and reports takes it is subject to the same set of principles. I emphasise here some specific principles in relation to this aspect of the social carer's work.

Essential principles of recording and report writing
Confidentiality

Individual service user records and reports should be regarded as confidential information, accessible only to the service user and those authorised to read them. For this reason they should be kept in a safe place which is locked when records are not in use, for example in a filing cabinet in the agency office.

Anti-discriminatory practice

Recording and report writing are parts of practice and so embody this principle as much as any other part of the social care worker's task. Ahmad (1990) emphasised that reports should address culture in a constructive way and provide people with the opportunity to present their own perspectives.

Objectivity and accuracy

This means the avoidance of subjective opinion, prejudice, preconceived ideas and impressions. It is in the nature of recording that it is a selection of what has occurred and this needs to be acknowledged. The worker needs to ensure that what is recorded is as factually accurate as possible. Checking accuracy with the service user, and both user and worker signing the record once the content has been agreed, is one possible safeguard.

Functions of recording and report writing

Recording and report writing serve many different functions.

Exercise 1

Before reading further, jot down what you think of as the functions of recording and report writing and compare it with the list which follows.

A group of social care workers felt that recording and report writing served the following functions:

- to improve the service user's quality of life

- to keep staff informed

- to maintain continuity

- to evaluate progress

- to protect the service user and the worker

- to make staff accountable

- to monitor what is happening

- to write down appointments and ensure they are kept

- to discuss in supervision

- to fulfil agency requirements

- to record the process and decisions made in assessment, care planning and implementation

- to evaluate progress

Exercise 2

For many people the written word presents huge barriers. The barrier is broken down only by taking the bull by the horns and getting some practice, ensuring that the principles outlined above are strictly adhered to. To practise writing things down try the following:

1) Write a record of your work with one person during the course of one day. If possible share this with that person (or, if this is not possible, another worker or family member) and ask what he or she thinks of this.

2) Keep your own diary of the work you do

over the course of one month and, if possible, bring this to a supervision session with your workplace supervisor.

3) Write in detail about a piece of work which you found difficult, what you thought about the way you tackled it and how you might change your practice in relation to a similar situation in the future.

4) Contribute to agency records whenever you have the opportunity.

5) Write a report which can be used at a service user's review.

CASE EXAMPLE – MR WALLACE

This, though a fictional statement, has its basis in an actual record. A keyworker, who is helping to arrange a bus trip for a group of service users, writes the following in the daily report:

Today Mr Wallace once again lost his temper and stormed out of the dining room. He continues to be a difficult and unreasonable man who is frequently agitated. In my opinion it would be better for everyone if he didn't come on the coach trip next week.

If this short report is examined it has several shortcomings:

1) It contains the words 'difficult' and 'unreasonable' which can label Mr Wallace as a problem for evermore.
2) There is no suggestion of exploration of why Mr Wallace is behaving as he is.
3) It is opinionated and fails to be objective.
4) The solution is a negative one. There is no enquiry into how it might be possible for Mr Wallace to go on the coach trip.
5) It seems unlikely that this record was shared or discussed with Mr Wallace.

How can this record be improved upon? If the social care worker can find some space and time he or she might use this to develop thinking about Mr Wallace and write this down as an informal record. For example:

Mr Wallace has now been at the home for five weeks. He often sits alone in the lounge and on two occasions recently has lost his temper. On the first occasion he shouted at Mr Smith, with whom he shares a room, for making too much noise early in the morning. Today, when there was a lot of noise in the dining room, Mr Wallace banged his chair on the floor and left without eating his meal. It does seem that he prefers peace and quiet and he appears quite happy during the day to read his newspaper. He doesn't mix much with other service users. I think it might be an idea to explore this with Mr Wallace. There are times, apart from the above, when Mr Wallace is very agitated. He can't settle, says he feels angry, upset and unwell. I will talk to Mr Wallace about this and suggest keeping a diary together of the times when he is agitated: what happens just before them, how does he feel and how does he resolve them. The Home will be having a coach trip next week and Mr Wallace has said that he would like to come on it. We need to discuss how he might feel if there's a lot of noise on the coach or during the whole trip and how we can make the trip possible and enjoyable for him and everyone else.

But what if there is not time to write more than a few lines? How can this be summarised at the same time as escaping the pitfalls of the first report? For example:

Mr Wallace is still taking time to settle in and today he stormed out of the dining room. As with the last time he lost his temper it seems to have been set off by an unusual amount of noise. He is agitated too on occasion and I will suggest exploring this by keeping a diary. Mr Wallace wishes to come on the coach trip next week and we shall look at ways of making this possible and enjoyable for him and everyone else.

Exercise 3

Examine critically all three of these reports. Give your own views about them. What is good about them? What is poor about them? How would you improve on them? They all have at least one major shortcoming. What is it?

In spite of time constraints there is still a case for sometimes writing in detail, especially where there seem to be problems which need to be dealt with. This can be done in several ways. For example:

1) The service user can keep a diary. This gives an idea of what is important to him or her, records the ordinary as well as the extraordinary and gives the user's perspective.

2) A member of staff, such as a keyworker, if possible with the help of the service user, can keep a record for a set period of time, for example a week, of behaviour at particular times. For example, Mr Wallace's behaviour could be recorded at meal times. This may tell us that at most meals he is perfectly content and is only agitated if someone he does not much like sits next to him or there is more noise than usual associated with a disagreement. It will give information about the meals when he is all right and not in crisis, as well as the occasions when he bangs his chair on the floor and walks out.

3) A member of staff and service user can together compile a record which sets down general feelings and needs in order that planning can take place.

This sharing, or rather the absence of it, was one shortcoming which occurred in all three reports about Mr Wallace.

4) A record can be kept of incidents in order that they can be seen in their context: what preceded them, how they were dealt with and what were the consequences.

One great advantage of writing things down is that it does enable, indeed it forces, you to think about what you are writing about and hopefully reflect upon what is going on with a service user in his or her situation. This reflection is important because it can make the difference between practice based upon reason and planning and practice based upon routine and instinct. Routine and instinct have their place but do not usually result in improvements in service whereas reason, analysis, thinking and planning, combined with warmth, empathy and respect, can revolutionise it.

Recording systems

Where recording or report writing are formalised for a particular purpose, agencies usually devise a procedure for structuring the information recorded in order that it is easily understood and accessible. Here headings are useful, with different sections of a standardised form relating to different areas of information. Seed and Kaye (1994) in their summary needs assessment suggest the following summary headings:

- background and health

- social support needs

- interests, preferences and social network features

- present services

- implications and growth points

- agreed recommendations

This was written in relation to people with learning disabilities but can be easily adapted for use with anyone. Social services and social work departments have devised their own community care assessment forms for summarising all of the information relevant to needs. One which I examined has 18 sections, including important sections for the service user's views, the carer's views and the recording of differences or disagreements between service user/carer views. The trouble with forms is that they can not only be enabling but also limiting. If there is not a question in relation to an issue then people tend not to write about it. Forms therefore have to be carefully planned, to be seen as means and not ends and to be only one source of information.

Legislation

Since 1987 the Access to Personal Files Act has given people the right to see information held on them by social services, social work and housing departments. This applies to all manual files and records, although information about third parties (such as brothers and sisters) cannot be given without prior consent. This has some implications for the practice of writing reports, although if recording had always been in the service user's best interests these implications would hardly need stating. The purpose and content of records should be clear, ensuring that information is both relevant and accurate. Differences among facts, opinions and professional assessment should be made explicit. One of the most important implications is that recording is now encouraged to be much more open with maximum involvement by the service user, and with the ultimate goal of service users fully involved in the compilation of their own records and reports.

The second piece of relevant legislation is the Data Protection Act 1984, which gives protection to people in relation to information held in such a form that it can be processed by equipment operating automatically i.e. information which is held on computers. Those who hold this type of information must register with the Data Protection Register and must give people information kept about them. There are restrictions on access to certain types of information, one of these being information kept for the purposes, or acquired in the course of, carrying out social work, where it would be likely to cause serious harm to the physical, mental or emotional condition of the person applying for access. Under the Act the individual has the right to see information about him or herself held on computer, to complain if information is incorrect or

misleading and to have such information corrected or removed.

Recording and report writing are useful only in as far as the service user remains central to the process, and evaluating and optimising the user's quality of life are seen as the ultimate goals. The principles of confidentiality, anti-discriminatory practice, objectivity and accuracy are paramount. It is important to avoid the use of jargon and negative labels.

Suggestions for further reading

Three books already mentioned give some useful guidelines and information in relation to recording and report writing. These are:

- Coulshed, V. (1991) *Social Work Practice*. London: Macmillan.

- Seed, P. and Kaye, G. (1994) *Handbook for Assessing and Managing Care in the Community*. London: Jessica Kingsley.

- Ward, A. (1993) *Working in Group Care*. Birmingham: Venture Press.

11 | Evaluating and ending

In the light of the evaluation, shortcomings can be identified and, resources permitting, modifications made to improve subsequent care plans.

THOMSON, 1995, P 333.

As in other aspects of the work, it is the responsibility of team members both individually and collectively to work out appropriate ways of handling departure so that it can be used constructively rather than being denied or overlooked.

WARD, 1993, P 112.

This final chapter examines the importance of evaluating what you have done, of evaluating yourself, your values, attitudes, work; and of endings, how you finish things off, deal with goodbyes and with loss. This is also a chapter which returns to take a positive look at values and principles and their fundamental place as the foundation upon which all other work is built.

Evaluating your work and yourself

The process of thorough assessment, care planning and implementation is incomplete if the work done and your role are not also evaluated. Without this evaluation the worth of your work cannot be appraised. It is difficult, if not impossible, to make improvements in the light of experience without it. Evaluation means judging the worth and quality of

what you have done. In the light of this, changes can be made to care plans, to practice and to your approach to work in the future. How can this evaluation be achieved? Many avenues have been explored already in this book: supervision was examined in Chapter 8, staff meetings in Chapter 9, the value of writing things down and reflecting on practice were referred to in Chapter 10 and the value of diaries has been touched upon many times. Exercise 1 presents a useful set of questions to ask yourself in evaluating any work done. Below is a return to discussion of one form of evaluation, supervision, as an illustration of the evaluation process.

Supervision as a means of evaluating practice

Everyone needs supervision. No matter how perfect you think you are or how

Exercise 1

Take one piece of work and evaluate it by asking yourself the following questions:

1) Does it apply social care values and principles?

2) Does it achieve the goals which it set out to achieve?

3) Is the service user satisfied with the outcome? Are you? Are others in the user's network?

4) Were resources adequate?

5) If you were not completely happy with the result, was it because:

   – you were dissatisfied with your work?

   – there was a lack of collaboration?

   – there were inadequate resources?

   – there was not enough time?

   – other reasons?

6) In the light of your answers to these questions, would you do the same thing next time? If not, what would you change, how and why?

experienced you are, supervision adds an extra dimension to practice. It puts you in the position of explaining what you are doing, lets you discuss what you have done and gives someone else the opportunity to comment upon it in a constructive and helpful way. That is when you get it and it is good. If you do not get it or it is not good, fight for it. Remember the need for supervision and provide it

yourself when you are in a position to do so. Here are some things which could be discussed in supervision as part of the evaluation process. You could:

• Evaluate how effective you have been in meeting goals which have been set or agreed, for instance in terms of a care plan or a specific task such as organising an outing. One social care worker reflected on her work with two sisters in a children's home. It was not until her supervision session that she realised the significance of promoting visits to two older sisters in another unit and was confident enough to arrange for these visits to take place. The care plan had included maintaining links with family members but all attention had been focused upon maintaining contact with parents.

• Reflect on the way your attitudes, approaches and skills affect your relationship with and the behaviour of both service users and colleagues. One new worker in a drugs unit said in supervision that he felt angry with a service user when he did not turn up for an appointment. This affected his subsequent interview when the service user casually turned up two days later. His supervisor listened and explained the circumstances and lifestyles of many service users of the agency and encouraged the worker to accept the person and where *he* was rather than where the worker wanted him to be. After this discussion and the opportunity offered to voice his anger and disappointment the worker was calmer about missed appointments and more able to help and accept people from their own starting points.

- Understand how values, principles, attitudes and feelings can influence your practice. This can involve working through the values and principles of social care giving examples of how you have applied these. This can also include an examination of the influence of your own attitudes and beliefs. How would you feel if you were of one religious persuasion and you were asked to take someone to church who was of another? One social care worker faced with this situation felt that although she would previously have seen this as against her principles, she realised that on this occasion if she did not take the service user to church then no-one else would. She put herself in that person's shoes, realised how disappointed the user would be if she did not go and went along with her ... and enjoyed the experience. The care worker said that she had not previously considered how her values and attitudes might influence practice.

  One very positive example of how attitudes affect practice was given to me by a social care worker working in a home for elderly people. She had very positive attitudes towards maintaining family links and about special occasions. In supervision she received encouragement to put the following plan into action. George's eight-year-old granddaughter had a birthday coming up and she was visiting her grandfather, travelling a considerable distance to see him. Some ideas for her visit were suggested to George and he thought a surprise birthday party would be a wonderful idea. He was assisted by staff in planning this and went up to town with one member of staff to choose a present, decorations and food for the

occasion. Maximum choice and maximum participation by George were encouraged. On the day of the party staff helped George to decorate his room with balloons and the cook supplied sandwiches, cakes and biscuits. When Susan, the grandchild, arrived she was delighted with the party and her presents and she has some lovely photographs of her day with her grandfather. She thoroughly enjoyed herself, but if it had not been for the positive attitudes among staff and the encouragement received in supervision about encouraging family occasions this would never have taken place.

- In discussion with your supervisor, identify areas where you display particular strengths; also identify areas needing further development and how this is to be achieved. One supervisor observed a social care worker assisting with lunches in a home for elderly people. The worker informed service users individually of what was on offer e.g. fish or cold ham. Everyone was able to make a choice and did so. When the supervisor commented on this the worker responded that it just came automatically. The supervisor however praised the worker for respecting the service user's rights and possessing a commitment to providing good quality care. This is not automatic but a strength.

- Think about how supervision contributes to your good practice. Social care workers mentioned the following ways in which supervision can contribute to good practice:

  – it provides an opportunity to question practice and reflect upon it

– it can offer reassurance or guidance when you are not sure whether your practice was good or not

– it enables you to gain confidence e.g. in delegating tasks if you are just starting as a senior care worker

– it enables you to prioritise work more effectively

– it gives the opportunity to explore alternative ways of approaching or dealing with a specific situation.

One social care worker reflected that he had, one evening, promised a service user that he would return to talk to him 'later on'. For one reason or another he had been prevented from doing so. He had known all along that it would be difficult to find time to return. With his supervisor he explored how he might have coped with this differently in future. He decided that he would probably now have the confidence to say that he would do his best to get back to him later, rather than promising. By doing this the worker could continue to maintain a trusting relationship with the service user and protect himself from the guilt of not being able to keep a promise. The other solution is to ensure that the service user is seen again, but in reality this is not always a possibility.

Endings – how you finish things off, deal with goodbyes and with loss

There are many endings in social care: the end of a shift, the end of a job, the end of a person's stay or a person's life. All of these endings are significant events. Months of work can be completely ruined if the ending is not thought about, if what follows afterwards is not carefully planned and if its significance both for the service user and worker is underestimated. Endings can be both events in their own right and part of a transition from one place to another or one stage of life to another. Some endings are major events, others are common occurrences. The end of a shift can happen two or three times a day – moving from one unit to another or leaving a care establishment altogether may only happen once. Endings are as important as arrivals and beginnings.

Adrian Ward (1993) has written at some length about ending a shift. He divides the end into the three stages of preparation for leaving, departure and after departure, and emphasises that if departure is not carefully dealt with it can develop into a major problem. These three stages can equally apply to any ending and they are examined here in a general sense while giving examples which apply to particular occasions.

Preparation for leaving

In half an hour Diane will finish her shift as a social care worker in a home for elderly people. She is tired, it has been a long day, part of her would like to spend that 30 minutes smoking a cigarette and having a cup of tea . . . then she would like to walk out of the door and go for her bus. But even if she could do that she knows that a number of loose ends would be left untied:

• there is a short hand-over meeting to inform the on-coming shift about the events of the day

- she needs to write up her work with Mr James in the day book

- she said she would try to see Mrs Smith, who has been unwell, before she went home. She knows it will cheer her up if she just gives her a goodbye and a smile before she goes

- after the hand-over meeting there is usually an informal cup of tea when everyone can let off a bit of steam before they leave the building

- she nearly always pops into the Scott lounge to say goodnight. It would seem odd if she did not go.

The hand-over meeting is built into the shift and it is therefore necessary to attend unless there is a crisis going on; similarly, the day book must be completed. The cup of tea is optional, so is Mrs Smith and so is saying goodbye to the people in the Scott lounge. But Diane knows from experience that she always feels more stressed if she goes home without doing these things and knows too that it can take several days before some people will forgive her if she does not say goodbye. She feels it is worth the additional investment, and as she waits for the bus she is able to feel completion and the end of a shift well done.

The ending of a shift is a relatively small ending. What of the 'big' endings in social care: a teenager leaving care for independent living, an elderly person going from a residential home to a core and cluster project, a young adult with learning difficulties going to live in a hostel, an elderly man leaving his own home for residential care? These are all very different situations but they also have some similarities. They are significant events, they must be carefully planned if they are to be successful, they are all important transitions from one stage of life to another. Even though in all of these situations the aim is to improve the quality of life for the person involved, there are likely to be mixed feelings and there are probably both losses and gains. Social care workers need to be able to take on board the feelings of loss associated with change of any kind, to understand these feelings and to help people to come out on the other side in a healthy state. One way of improving the handling of loss and change is to understand the process. Many researchers (e.g. Worden, 1982) have looked at this process and below is a short summary of the tasks which may be involved in coping with changed circumstances:

- **Task 1** – acceptance of the reality of the change, its significance and the reasons for it. Sometimes people who are facing change or loss try to pretend that it is not happening or pretend that it does not matter to them or affect them in any way. The social care worker can assist by helping the person involved to appreciate that it is a reality and that it does matter. Communication skills of attentive listening and responding with acceptance and genuineness are important in enabling the service user to feel that his or her feelings are important. Once this task has been achieved Task 2 can be tackled.

- **Task 2** – to acknowledge and allow the feelings associated with loss and change. These feelings may be very mixed and could involve:

  – the pain of separation from relatives,

friends, carers and many others in the service user's network

– relief that a not very satisfactory period of life is over

– apprehension about the new situation

– anger that the change is happening at all

– excitement because the new situation has been long awaited and looked forward to.

Working through the feelings, especially the negative feelings, associated with change and loss can be greatly helped by someone who acknowledges that whatever the feelings are it is OK to express them. In situations of severe loss people sometimes feel that they are going completely mad, and they may feel physically unwell and extremely tired. Someone who understands that this can be all very 'normal' during a significant change and listens, responds and even comes up with appropriate practical help, can greatly assist towards the achievement of this task in order that Task 3 can be tackled.

• **Task 3** – to adjust to a new situation and/or a new environment. This is more about beginnings than endings. The service user may now have left one place for another or may be living in different circumstances but in the same place. There is possibly a new set of workers who will deal with the feelings associated with this task or the same workers may continue. Often Tasks 1 and 2 remain incomplete. During Task 3 social care

workers need to appreciate what a service user may have been through, to see the change as significant and to enable as full an adjustment as possible through the use of all of the values and skills in his or her repertoire. Only when there has been a recognition and acceptance of changed circumstances, a redefinition of what life is now going to be about, and a careful and shared process of assessment and planning in terms of the new situation, can the service user get on with maximum fulfilment in the face of changed circumstances and/or a new environment.

• **Task 4** – investment in the changed situation but with continuing links with significant networks. This is the stage of participation in the new situation and an acceptance of it. It does not mean severing links with other networks but involves emotional investment in *this* situation rather than the one which existed before. Progress in the task can be hindered by hanging on to the past rather than being able to accept changed circumstances and move on to the future. If the first three tasks have been completed successfully then tackling this one is a natural progression.

Sometimes, however, people come into a new care situation with all sorts of unresolved feelings spilling over from departures, losses and changes which have not been dealt with very well in the past. What are some of the things which can be done to ensure that this does not happen to those who are leaving you and that the tasks associated with change and loss can be completed successfully? Some of these things are mentioned above: the value of good communication, the use of counselling skills, the value of careful planning, an understanding of the meaning, significance and the tasks associated with loss and change.

Exercise 2

Imagine that a 13-year-old girl is leaving a children's home in order to live with foster parents. Can you identify eight things you would do in preparation for this departure?

Your account may well be much fuller than the one which follows, but here are some suggestions:

1) Build in preparation for leaving right from the beginning, be realistic in discussing possibilities and gain a full picture of the young person's preferences.

2) Collaborate with the young person, her family, her network, other agencies and professional workers. Also work with a team approach so that all team members are part of the leaving process.

3) Ensure that the departure is as carefully planned as possible and that discussion of it is not delayed until it becomes unavoidable.

4) Provide opportunities for the young person to discuss her feelings about the departure, what this means to her, what she feels about the future and anything else she wants to talk about.

5) Try to make the process of leaving a gradual one with preparation visits to the new foster home on an increasingly regular basis, perhaps with some two or three-day stays beforehand.

6) Plan a party and a farewell present from both the other young people and the staff. This marks the occasion as significant and gives a pleasant occasion for saying goodbyes. It provides happy memories too.

7) Leave the door open for return visits if this is possible. Most endings need not be totally final things and it should be possible to take forward some of the past into the future.

8) Do not avoid saying goodbye and do not avoid facing the change with the young person, since this approach can contribute to a lack of adjustment to her new situation.

These are just a few suggestions. You may feel that you have better ones or would not deal with this situation in the same way at all. The important thing is that you have thought about it and will, hopefully, think about the best way to tackle future departures and changes.

And finally . . .

Well, now where do you go? You go back to the beginning, back to the value base and back to an emphasis on the importance of placing the person at the centre of everything that social care is about. Social care is not for the benefit of the social care worker but of the service user. Respect for the worth and dignity of all individuals and the promotion of social justice are at the core of this work. Where there is poor practice it is usually because it rests upon poor foundations. Where the value base is not sound and where communication is lacking the structure which is social care comes tumbling down. Where they are strong and sound the possibilities are endless.

Afterword

Communication

There's something to be said for communication after all;
Sometimes wordless, sometimes babbling on like a river,
We connect ourselves to that threatening world outside
And avoid the abyss of total aloneness.

Feelings, needs, dislikes and likes,
I can tell you all of these, or not, as I choose.
I can sit here silent and rigid
Communicating to you my distress.

Tomorrow

Live in hope.
Tomorrow will be a better day.
Perhaps tomorrow
Jane won't decorate the wall with her mashed potato,
Tom won't wander off and steal a bicycle.
There won't be pandemonium
As once more John is returned by the police
Only to disappear again that same afternoon.

Tomorrow everything we try will work.
We shall continue to ignore Jane's misdemeanours
And praise her small achievements.
She will get the message
And behave herself.
Tom will realise that we care for him and
Love him and that he has a bicycle.
He doesn't need to steal another one.
John, you don't need to be anyone but yourself.
You're a fine lad but please stay.
We can't help you if you're not here.
Yes, tomorrow will be a better day.

The Social Carer

We had a social carer once,
We could talk to 'er all day.
She'd arrive first thing in't morning,
We'd save loads a' stuff to say.

She'd come in like the sunshine,
Beaming cheerful and bright,
And ask how we was feeling.
We could tell she meant it right.

And then we had a silent one,
Hadn't a word t' say.
Gloom and doom we called 'er.
She'd really ruin our day.

Miserable as sin she was.
God knows what made 'er tick.
We tried to cheer 'er up a bit.
It was like talking to a brick.

That one handed in 'er notice,
Or perhaps she got the sack.
And Oh what a relief it is,
They're sending the old one back.

Glossary

Acceptance Taking people as they are without judging them; an absence of rejection.

Adult Training Centre (ATC) A day unit usually for people with learning disabilities at which service users are encouraged, enabled and empowered to fulfil physical, social, emotional and intellectual potential. The term 'day centre' is now often replacing the term 'ATC'.

Advising Telling others how they might act, feel or think rather than letting them decide for themselves.

Advocacy Actively promoting and representing the cause of another; speaking on behalf of someone as if speaking *as* that person.

Agency An establishment or organisation providing a service to service users.

Assessment An exploration of service user needs as part of the process of care, in order to enable the user to reach a quality of life which is as good as it can be.

Behavioural work A way of helping people to change behaviours which are reducing their quality of life, through techniques based upon learning theory.

Body language Non-verbal communication expressed through the position, attitude and expression of the body, or parts of the body e.g. the way you sit, the degree of eye contact; what you say with your body rather than in words.

Care plan An agreement arising from an assessment about what needs are to be met, how they are to be achieved and how problems are to be dealt with.

Choice Promoting choice means giving different options, real options, from which the service user can select as independently as possible.

Client The recipient or user of a service; this term is still currently used in counselling but is being replaced by the term 'service user' in social care.

Communication Communication occurs whenever people receive and/or give messages which they regard as significant. It can be verbal, non-verbal or symbolic.

Community care Providing the services and support which people need to be able to live as independently as possible in their own homes or in 'homely' settings in the community.

Confidentiality Maintaining the right to privacy of information; not divulging personal information unless given permission to do so by the service user, except in some extreme situations where information must be divulged by law.

Congruence Being genuine and not pretending; having and being seen to have your thoughts, feelings, words and actions match each other.

Core and cluster A form of community care in which service users live in groups of apartments or houses (clusters) in a neighbourhood supported from a central support system (the core).

Counselling A process which aims to help people to help themselves by making better choices and by becoming better decision makers.

Empathy Putting yourself in someone else's shoes and attempting to imagine how he or she feels.

Empowerment Enabling people to take control of their lives; gaining the power to make decisions and choices.

Evaluation Appraising the worth and quality of work done.

Genuineness Sincerity, congruence and a lack of pretence.

Group A plurality of persons who have a common identity, at least some feeling of unity, certain common goals and shared norms.

Group work Working with a group of people towards achieving stated goals.

Grouping A gathering of people but without an identity as a group.

HNC Higher National Certificate, granted by an awarding body such as BTEC or SCOTVEC upon completion of an approved training course which usually includes substantial practical experience.

HND Higher National Diploma; usually a two-year full-time course which can be an extension of an HNC.

Holistic care Care which sees the whole person in a social situation and attempts to satisfy physical, intellectual, communication, emotional, cultural and social needs.

Implementation Putting plans into effect; carrying out what has been agreed upon in the planning process.

Institutionalisation Becoming dependent upon the routines and narrow confines of an institution resulting in such characteristics as apathy, lack of initiative and inability to make personal plans.

Keyworker A worker who is allocated to work more closely with a service user than other workers and who has a co-ordinating role with that service user within the agency.

Labelling Referring to acts or conditions by attaching a (usually negative) name to them which then becomes a 'master status', e.g. labelling people as deviant, neurotic or difficult.

Legislation The law; acts of Parliament.

Modelling Demonstrating behaviour, feelings or thoughts to others which may, if adopted, improve the quality of life for the service user.

Monitoring On-going evaluation; keeping a check on what you are doing to ensure that it meets objectives.

Non-verbal communication The music behind the words; communication not using language; includes facial expression, body movement and eye contact.

Normalisation Affording all citizens the same rights and opportunities to develop and contribute to society in ways which are socially valued; developed predominantly as an attempt to promote the aim of integrating disabled people fully into society.

NVQ National Vocational Qualification; awarded at different levels upon successful completion of a detailed assessment of practice by an approved workplace assessor.

Principle Rule of conduct, especially right conduct; the practical manifestation of values, relating to everyday practice.

Private sector That part of provision which is run, usually on a for-profit basis, by companies or individuals; part of the mixed economy of care under the National Health Service and Community Care Act 1990; not voluntary organisation or statutory provision.

Psychology The science and study of human behaviour.

Record A written account of significant information including decisions, incidents, feelings, actions and monitoring of assessments/care plans.

Relationship Being connected in some way with another; a helping relationship is characterised by empathy, genuineness and unconditional positive regard.

Residential care The provision for need in a registrable home. Under the Registered Homes Act 1984 a registrable home is one which provides board and personal care for four or more people who need such care by reason of age, disablement, past or present dependence on alcohol or drugs or present mental disorder.

Respite care A temporary period usually spent in a supported, residential environment in order to give carers a break and/or to provide help and a change for those in need of care. It can also be used as an opportunity for assessment or re-assessment.

Role playing Enacting behaviour in simulated settings or in imagination.

Scapegoats Individuals or groups of people who have been inaccurately and unjustly targeted as being responsible for a problem.

Self esteem A sense of your own worth. This can be a positive or negative evaluation of yourself.

Service user One who avails him or herself of help or assistance towards fulfilling need and/or improving the quality of life; sometimes also called a client or a resident.

Social care Aims to enhance the quality of people's lives through a balance of practical help and the provision of opportunities to meet physical, intellectual, communication, emotional, cultural and social needs.

Social work Concerned primarily to assist people considered to be at risk or in need of specific intervention in their lives; also increasingly involved in care management. Social work and social care share the same value base and also many methods and skills. There is no clear-cut dividing line between the two.

Statutory Provided by central or local government.

Stigma A distinguishing mark or characteristic which is both noticeable and objectionable; a mark of disgrace or infamy. Stigmas have the power to spoil a person's social and personal identity.

Summarising Making statements which say briefly what you or another person has been saying; may include feedback from you.

Support Giving encouragement, help, understanding, warmth, whatever is needed, to another.

SVQ Scottish Vocational Qualification; awarded at different levels upon successful completion of a detailed assessment of practice by an approved workplace assessor.

Symbolic communication Messages, behaviour and actions which represent something else e.g. an unwelcoming physical environment says 'we don't care about you'.

Task-centred work Time limited, focused, short-term work which aims to achieve agreed tasks; can be used in dealing with a variety of problems.

Team A group of people who work together to achieve the philosophy and goals of their agency.

Transitions Changes which people undergo during their lives: for example marriage, the loss of a partner or retirement.

Value That which is desirable or worthy for its own sake.

Voluntary organisation A not-for-profit, non-statutory organisation; often a charity.

References

Ahmad, A. (1990) *Practice with Care*. London: Race Equality Unit/National Institute for Social Work.

Ainsworth, F. and Fulcher, L. (eds) (1981) *Group Care for Children*. London: Tavistock.

Audit Commission Report (1986) *Making a Reality of Community Care*. London: HMSO.

Ball, L. and Soura, T. in Brown, A. and Clough, R. (eds) (1989) *Groups and Groupings, Life and Work in Day and Residential Centres*. London: Tavistock/Routledge.

Barclay Report, (1982) *Social Workers: Their Roles and Tasks*. London: Bedford Square Press.

Beresford, P. and Treillion, S. (1995), 'Careful Collaboration'. *Community Care* magazine, 27 July–2 August 1995. Haywards Heath: Reid Business Publishing.

Blakemore, K. and Drake, R. (eds) (1996) *Understanding Equal Opportunities Policies*. London: Prentice Hall.

Bowlby, J., Fry, M., Ainsworth, M. (1965) *Child Care and the Growth of Love*, 2nd edn. Geneva: World Health Organisation.

Brandon, D. in Ramon, S. (1991) *Beyond Community Care*. London: Macmillan in association with Mind Publications.

Brearley, C.P. (1977) *Residential Work with the Elderly*. London: Routledge and Kegan Paul.

British Association of Counselling (1985) *Counselling: Definition of Terms in Use with Expansion and Rationale*. Rugby: British Association for Counselling.

Brown, A. and Clough, R. (eds.) (1989) *Groups and Groupings, Life and Work in Day and Residential Centres*. London: Tavistock/Routledge.

Bull, D. (1982) *Welfare Advocacy: Whose Means to What Ends?* Birmingham: BASW Publications.

Bulmer, M. (1987) *The Social Basis of Community Care*. London: Allen and Unwin.

Campbell, J. (1995) 'Thirty Years War', *Community Care* magazine: 7–13 December 1995. Haywards Heath: Reid Business Publishing.

Caplan, G. (1961) *Prevention of Mental Disorders in Children*. New York: Basic Books.

Centre for Policy on Ageing (1996) *A Better Home Life*. London: Centre for Policy on Ageing.

Civikly, J. (1981) *Contexts of Communication*. New York: Holt, Reinhart and Winston.

Clough, R. (1987) *Scandals in Residential Centres, An Unpublished Report for the Wagner Committee*. University of Bristol.

Community Care magazine, 22 December 1994. 'Neglect Forces Home Closure.' Haywards Heath: Reid Business Publishing.

Coulshed, V. (1991) *Social Work Practice. An Introduction*, 2nd edn. London: Macmillan.

Craig, M. (1979) *Blessings*. London: Hodder & Stoughton.

Crompton, M. (1990) *Attending to Children*. London: Edward Arnold (a member of the Hodder Headline Group).

Crompton, M. (1992) *Children and Counselling*. London: Edward Arnold (a member of the Hodder Headline Group).

Davidson, J. (1995) 'The Art of Social Care'. Unpublished. Glasgow: Cardonald College.

Davis, L. (1992) *Social Care, Rivers of Pain, Bridges of Hope*. London: Whiting and Birch.

Department of Health (1989) *Caring for People. Community Care in the next decade and beyond*. London: HMSO.

Donohue, E. (1985) *Echoes in the Hills*. Surbiton: Social Care Association Publications.

Douglas, T. (1978) *Basic Groupwork*. London: Routledge.

Egan, G. (1986) *The Skilled Helper*. Monteray: Brooks/Cole.

Elkan, R. and Kelly, D. (1991) *A Window in Homes*. Surbiton: Social Care Association (Education).

Employment Development Group (1994), *Equal Opportunities Directory*. London: EDG.

Goffman, E. (1961) *Asylums: Essays on the Social Situations of Mental Patients and Other Inmates*. New York: Doubleday.

Griffiths, D. (1991) *Politics of Health*. Fenwick, Ayrshire: Pulse Publications.

Griffiths, Sir R. (1988) *Community Care: Agenda for Action*. London: HMSO.

Haralambos, M. (1995) *Sociology: themes and perspectives*, 4th edn. London: Collins Educational.

Harris, J. and Kelly, D. (1991) *Management Skills in Social Care*. Aldershot: Gower.

Hemingway, J. (1987) *Where There's a Will*. London: Video Arts.

Henwood, M. (1995) 'Measure for Measure'. *Community Care* magazine, 6–12 July 1995. Haywards Heath: Reid Business Publishing.

HMSO (1984) *Data Protection Act*. London.

HMSO (1990) *National Health Service and Community Care Act*. London.

HMSO (1987) *Personal Files Act*. London.

HMSO (1976) *Race Relations Act*. London.

HMSO (1975) *Sex Discrimination Act*. London.

Hough, M. (1994) *A Practical Approach to Counselling*. London: Pitman Publishing.

Huczynski, A. and Buchanan, D. (1991) *Organizational Behaviour*. London: Prentice Hall.

Hudson, B.L. and Macdonald, G.M. (1986) *Behavioural Social Work: An Introduction*. London: Macmillan.

Inskipp, F. (1988) *Counselling Skills*. Cambridge: National Extension College.

Jones, K., Brown, J. and Bradshaw, J. (1978) *Issues in Social Policy*. London: Routledge and Kegan Paul.

Jones, M. (1971) *Small Group Psychotherapy*. London: Penguin.

Kahan, B. (1994) *Growing up in Groups*. London: HMSO.

Kelly, J. (1981) *A Philosophy of Communication*. London: The Centre for the Study of Communication and Culture.

Kina, Lady Avebury, Chairperson of Working Party sponsored by the Department of Health and Social Security (1984) *Home Life: A Code of Practice for Residential Care*. Centre for Policy on Ageing.

Kirby, P. (1995) *A Word from the Street*. Wallington: Community Care.

Lishman, J. (1994) *Communication in Social Work*. London: Macmillan.

Lishman, J. (1991) *Handbook of Theory for Practice Teachers in Social Work*. London: Jessica Kingsley.

Lynch, B., Perry, R. (1992) *Experiences of Community Care*. Harlow: Longman.

MacIver, R., Page, C. (1961) *Society: An Introductory Analysis*. London: Macmillan.

McGee, J. (1990) 'Gentle Teaching: the basic tenet,' *Nursing Times* 86: 32, 68–72.

Mallinson, I. (1995) *Keyworking in Social Care*. London: Whiting and Birch.

Marchant, C. (1994), 'Losing Out.' *Community Care* magazine 22 December 1994. Haywards Heath: Reid Business Publishing

Meredith, B. (1993) *The Community Care Handbook*. London: ACE books (a publication of Age Concern).

Miller, J. and Grant, J. (1972) *Assessment of Elderly People for Residential Care*. London: Annual Review of the Residential Care Association.

Murphy, D. (1987) *Tales from Two Cities*. London: John Murray.

National Institute for Social Work (1988) *Residential Care, the Research Reviewed*. London: HMSO.

Nelson-Jones, R. (1993) *Practical Counselling and Helping Skills*, 3rd edn. London: Cassell.

Novan, A. (1994) *Collaboration in Community Care in the 1990s*. London: Business Education Publishers.

Nursing Times, 10 March 1989. 'Berkshire Support Team.'

Open University (1990) K668 Workbook, *Communication: Participating in Social Relationships*. Prepared by A. Brechin and J, Swain, Milton Keynes: The Open University.

Owens, R. (1984) *Language Development: an Introduction*. Spronfield: Charles Merrill.

Oxfam UK and Ireland (1994) *The Oxfam Gender Training Manual*. Oxford: Oxfam.

Patti, R.J. (1971) 'Limitations and Prospects of Internal Advocacy.' *Social Casework* 55 (9), pp 537–45.

Payne, M. (1993) *Social Care in the Community*. London: Macmillan.

Pavlov, I. (1927) *Conditioned Reflexes*. Oxford: Oxford University Press.

Perlman, H. (1970) *Social Casework: A Problem-Solving Process*. Chicago: Chicago University Press.

Philpot, T. (ed.) (1989) *The Residential Opportunity, The Wagner Report and After*. Wallington: Community Care.

Portch, M. (1995) *Communication and Interpersonal Skills for Health and Social Care*. London: Hodder & Stoughton.

Powell, G. (1994) *Gender and Diversity in the Workplace – Learning Activities and Exercises*. Thousand Oaks, California: Sage.

Ramon, S. (ed.) (1991) *Beyond Community Care*. London: Macmillan in association with Mind publications.

Redl, F., Wineman, D. (1957) *The Aggressive Child*. The Free Press of Glencoe.

Reid, W. and Epstein, L. (eds.) (1977) *Task-Centred Practice*. New York: Columbia University Press.

Residential Forum (1996) *Creating a Home from Home*. Available from Surbiton: Social Care Association.

Rogers, C. (1991) *Client-Centred Therapy*. London: Constable.

Rogers, J. (1990) *Caring for People, Help at the Frontline*. Milton Keynes: Open University.

Rose, D. (1996) 'All in the Mind.' *Community Care* magazine, 4–10 April 1996. Haywards Heath: Reid Business Publishing.

Seed, P. (1990) *Introducing Network Analysis in Social Work*. London: Jessica Kingsley.

Seed, P. and Kaye, G. (1994) *Handbook for Assessing and Managing Care in the Community*. London: Jessica Kingsley.

Social Care Association (1994) *Code of Practice for Social Care*. Surbiton: Social Care Association.

Social Care Association (1991) *Keyworking in Social Care. An Introductory Guide*. Surbiton: Social Care Association.

Social Care Association (March 1993) *The Social Care Task: Improving the Quality of Life*. Surbiton: Social Care Association.

Social Care Association (1994) *Supervision in Social Care*. Surbiton: Social Care Association.

Stevenson, O. and Parsloe, P. (1993) *Community Care and Empowerment*. York: Joseph Rowntree Foundation in association with Community Care.

Thompson, N. (1993) *Anti-Discriminatory Practice*. London: Macmillan.

Thomson, H. (*et al.*) (1995) *Health and Social Care for Advanced GNVQ*, 2nd edn. London: Hodder & Stoughton.

Tomlinson, D. (1991) *Utopia, Community Care and the Retreat from the Asylums*. Milton Keynes: Open University Press.

Townsend, P. (1962) *The Last Refuge*. London: Routledge and Kegan Paul.

Tuckman, B.W. (1965) 'Developmental Sequences in Small Groups.' *Psychological Bulletin* 63 (6).

Turton, P. and Orr, J. (1993) *Learning to Care in the Community*, 2nd edn. London: Edward Arnold (a member of the Hodder Headline group).

Video Arts (1987) *Where There's a Will.* London: Video Arts.

Wagner, G. (1988) *Residential Care, A Positive Choice.* London: HMSO.

Ward, A. (1993) *Working in Group Care.* Birmingham: Venture Press.

Waterside Education and Training (1994) *Promoting Equality in Care Practice.* Produced and distributed by Sage and Hunt Printing Ltd, Andover: Association for Social Care Training.

Webb, R. and Tossell, D. (1991) *Social Issues for Carers. A Community Care Perspective.* London: Edward Arnold (a member of the Hodder Headline group).

Wheal, A. in collaboration with Buchanan, A. (1994) *Answers: A Handbook for Residential and Foster Carers of Young People aged 11–18 years.* Harlow: Longman.

Willmott, P. and Young, M. (1962) *Family and Kinship in East London.* London: Penguin.

Wistow, G., Knapp, M., Hardy, B., and Allen, C. (1994) *Social Care in a Mixed Economy.* Buckingham: Open University Press.

Wolfensberger, W. (1972) *The Principle of Normalization in Human Services.* Toronto: National Institute on Mental Retardation.

Worden, J.W. (1983) *Grief Counselling and Grief Therapy.* London: Tavistock Publications.

Index

ABC model 79–80
abuse, right to protection from 2, 18–19, 28
acceptance 2, 17, 18, 20
    of change or loss 138
Access to Personal Files Act (1987) 132–3
active listening 54–5, 57, 58
activities 108–9
activity groups 94
actualising tendency 59
advocacy 91–3
Ahmad, A. 129
Ainsworth, F. 84, 100
anti-discriminatory practice 21, 28–34
    equal opportunities policies 32–3
    recording and report writing 129
    and teamwork 28–9, 118
assessment
    asking questions 67
    and care planning 2, 4, 7, 72–6
    case examples 71–2
    checklists 66–7
    and community care 40
    defining 62
    diaries 67–8
    forms 66
    full and partial 63–4
    group discussions 70–1
    needs-led 40, 62–3, 65, 73
    network analysis 68
    observation 67
    as part of a model of care 64, 65
    personal history flowcharts 68–70
    photographs and pictures as tools in 72
    service-led 40, 62–3, 65
    and shared activities 71
    summary needs profile 66
attitudes, influence on practice 136
Audit Commission Report, *Making a Reality of Community Care* 38–9
autonomy 111

Ball, Lucy 97
Barclay Report 36, 111
bed times 108
behavioural work 77–84, 110, 111
    consequences 79–81
    modelling 81–2, 107, 110
    and Pavlov's dogs 78–9

thoughts and feelings 72–4
bereavement groups 93–4, 96, 97–9
Beresford, P. 113
Blakemore, K. 32
body language 59
Bowlby, J. 37
Brandon, David 12
Brearley, C.P. 72
British Association for Counselling (BAC) 55–6
Brown, A. 93, 97
Buchanan, D. 32
Bull, D. 91
Bulmer, M. 37

Campbell, Jane 42
Canada 12
Caplan, G. 84
care agreement 72
care environment *see* environment
care maintenance and therapeutic environment 100, 107–11
care managers, and assessment 63
care planning 2, 4, 7, 72–6
    case examples 74–6
    full and partial 74
    implementing care plans 77–99
    and resources 73–4
carers, support for 39
Caring for People (White Paper) 36, 39
case advocacy 91
cause advocacy 91–2
Centre for Policy on Ageing 15
centres for independent living (CILs) 42
chaining 80
challenging skills 60
change, adjusting to 138–40
children, conveying warmth to 54
choice 110–11
    and assessment 64
    and community care projects 41
    and counselling 56
    promotion of 2, 19, 21, 28
    and risk taking 20
CILs (centres for independent living) 42
citizen advocacy 92–3
Civikly, J. 45
client-centred counselling 58–9

Clough, R. 93, 97, 111
co-working 113, 114, 120–2
collaborative work 2, 103–4, 113–26
    outside the agency 122–4
    skills of 113–16
communication 2, 45–52, 139, 143
    and assessment 64, 65
    and co-keyworking 121
    and collaborative work 113–14, 115
    and constructive use of time 105
    defining 45
    enjoyment in 46, 47
    enthusiasm in 46, 47
    examples of good 48–51
    and hierarchies 50, 51
    non-verbal 46–8, 51, 52, 53
    Oomph factor in 46, 47, 122
    with outside agencies 122, 123
    and positive feelings 9
    symbolic 46–8, 51
    time for 51–2
    and the Tyn-y-Pwll residential project 49–50
    verbal 46–8, 51, 53
    and written records 127
    see also relationships
community care 2, 35–44
    and care agreements 72–3
    centres for independent living (CILs) 42
    and collaboration 123–4
    as a concept 35–7
    core and cluster projects 40–2, 123–4
    day centres 42–3
    and deinstitutionalisation 37
    and demographic change 38
    and drugs 38
    and family relationships 37–8
    funding 42, 44
    and local authorities 39–40
    mixed economy of care 39, 40, 43
    multi-disclipinary approach to 126
    needs-led assessment 40, 62–3
    and normalisation 38, 41, 43–4
    planning of 40
    and public attitudes 44
    resource centres 43–4
    service-led assessment 40, 62–3
    see also National Health Service and
        Community Care Act (1990)
Community Care magazine 15, 18, 42
community environment 100, 111
community police 123
confidentiality
    and assessment 64
    maintaining 2, 17–18

    of records and reports 128
congruence 53, 58–9
consequences of behaviour 79–81
core and cluster project 40–2
Coulshed, V. 84, 85, 127
counselling 52, 55–61, 110, 139
    core conditions of 58–9
    defining 55–6
    person-centred model of 56, 58–9
    skills of 56–8
    on the spot 58
    summarising 57, 59
    three stage skills model of 56, 59–60
critical incident analysis 83
cultural sensitivity 55

daily routines 107
Data Protection Act (1984) 133
Davidson, Jim 48
day centres 42–3
day planners 49, 52
deaf people 34, 48–9
dedication 46, 47
dependency 8–9
diaries 67–8, 128, 129–30, 131
difficult behaviour 7
discrimination 24–34
    and collaborative work 113–14
    and cultural sensitivity 55
    direct 26–7
    indirect 27
    institutional 27–8
    and lack of knowledge 25–6, 30–1
    and lack of understanding 26, 31
    legal redress against 28
    and prejudice 25, 26–7, 28–9
    unconscious 27
    see also anti-discriminatory practice
Donoghue, Edward 49–50
Douglas, T. 70, 93
Drake, R. 32

Egan, G. 56, 59
Elkan, R. 111
empathy 8, 9, 16
    and counselling 58, 59
    and relationships 52–3, 54
empowerment 2, 4, 7, 19, 21, 28, 111
    and advocacy 91
    and assessment 64
    and counselling 56
    and keyworking 13
    and risk taking 20
endings 95–6, 137–40

environment 100–12
  care maintenance and therapeutic 100,
    107–11
  community 100, 111
  organisational 100, 102–7
  physical 100, 101–2
Epstein, L. 85
equal opportunities policies 32–3
evaluation 2, 64, 115, 134–7
exemplary advocacy 93
exploitation, right to protection from 2,
  18–19, 28

family relationships 37–8, 111
feelings, behavioural work on 72–4
flexibility 114, 115
friendships 111
Fulcher, L. 84, 100
fulfilment 2, 21–2, 28, 59

Gender and Diversity in the Workplace 30
gentle teaching 84, 111
genuineness 52, 54, 59
getting up in the morning 107
goal setting 60
Goffman, Erving 10, 37
Grant, J. 63
Griffiths, Sir R. 35, 37, 38, 39
group care 4
group discussions 70–1
group work 93–9, 110
  activity groups 94
  advantages of 96–9
  bereavement groups 93–4, 96, 97–9
  co-working 121
  ending 95–6
  forming 94–5
  groups and groupings 93–4
  intermediate treatment projects 97
  norming 95
  performing 95
  reminiscence groups 96–7
  storming 95, 97
  see also teamwork

Haralambos, M. 64
Harris, John 105
Hemingway, J. 106
Henwood, Melanie 73
hierarchies 50, 51, 121
holidays 109
holistic approach to care 76, 113
homosexuality, and discrimination 25, 26
hospices 76, 124, 126

host organisations, collaboration with 122–3
Huczynski, A. 32
Hudson, B.L. 79, 84

independence 20, 44
individualisation 16, 21
institutional neurosis 10–11
institutionalisation 8, 9–10, 19
  and community care 37
  and the physical environment 101
integration policies 12
intermediate treatment projects 97
internal advocacy 92

Jones, Maxwell 37

Kahan, B. 100
Kaye, G. 66, 68, 132
Kelly, D. 105, 111
Kelly, J. 45
keyworking 8, 12–14
  co-keyworking 121–2

Lancaster, Ellen 46, 47
language differences, and
    communication 50–1
learning difficulties, people with
  assessment of 63, 66–7, 72
  resource centre for 43–4
learning theory 77–84
Lishman, J. 46, 48, 84
listening 54–5, 56–7
local authorities, and community care 39–40
Lynch, B. 42

Macdonald, G.M. 79, 84
McGee, J. 84
McIver, R. 36
magazine pictures 72
Mallinson, I. 121
management
  by walking about 106
  effective 105–6
meal times 107–8
meetings 109–10
  team meetings 116, 117–20
Miller, J. 63
modelling behaviour 81–2, 107, 110
multi-disciplinary work 114, 124–6
multiple oppressions 25
Murphy, Dervla 55

National Health Service and Community Care
  Act (1990) 35, 36, 38–40, 42, 44

National Health Service – *cont.*
  and assessment 62–3
  and the physical environment 101
  and resources 74
needs-led assessment 40, 62–3, 65
negative assumptions/attitudes 27, 29
negative feelings 8–9
neglect, right to protection from 18–19, 28
negotiation 114, 115
neighbourhood care schemes 37
network analysis 68
networks
  continuing links with 139
  developing 85–90, 110
non-verbal communication 46–8, 51, 52, 53
normalisation 8, 11–12
  and community care 38, 41, 43–4

observation 67
on the spot counselling 58
Oomph factor in communication 46, 47, 122
organisational environment 100, 102–7
Owens, R. 45
Oxfam Gender Training Manual 30

Page, C. 36
paraphrasing 57, 59
Parsloe, P. 19
partnership 114, 115–16
Patti, R.J. 91
Pavlov's dogs 78–9
Perlman, H. 45
Perry, R. 42
person-centred model of counselling 56,
  58–9
personal history flowcharts 68–70
photographs 72
physical environment 100, 101–2
Portch, M. 48
positive feelings 9
positive self-disclosure 60
positive self-disposition 46, 47
potential, maximising individual 2, 20–1, 28,
  43
prejudice 25, 26–7, 28–9
principles 15–16, 17–21
  of assessment 64
  and counselling 56
privacy 2, 17
private practice 117
psychiatric patients, and community care 37,
  38

quality, in community care projects 40

questions
  in assessment 67
  in counselling 57–8, 59
  open and closed 57–8

Ramon, Shulamit 12
records and reports 2, 127–33
  diaries 67–8, 128, 129–30, 131
  formal and informal records 128
  functions of 129–32
  incident reports 128
  legislation 132–3
  maintaining confidentiality 18
  objectivity and accuracy 129
  recording systems 132
Redl, F. 110
reflective responding 57
Reid, W. 85
relationships 52–5
  being genuine 52, 54, 59
  and collaborative work 113–14
  and empathy 52–3, 54
  and responsiveness 54–5
  showing warmth 53–4
  see also communication
reminiscence groups 96–7
reports *see* records and reports
residential care 39–40, 41
Residential Forum 15
resource centres 43–4, 111
resources, and care planning 73–4
respect for individuals 16, 21, 140
rights, and assessment 64
risk taking 2, 4, 20
Rogers, Carl 53–4, 56, 58–9
Rogers, J. 1
role play 30, 82
Rose, Diana 44

Seed, P. 66, 68, 86, 132
self advocacy 91
self concept 10
self disclosure 60
self worth, promoting 8
self-esteem 16, 21, 55
  and counselling 60
service users 6–8
  access to records 132–3
  and anti-discriminatory practice 28
  and co-keyworking 121
  and dependency 8–9
  diaries 68
  institutionalisation 8, 9–10, 19
  and team meetings 116, 117, 118

service-led assessment   40, 62–3, 65
shared activities   71
shifts
   ending   137–8
   and team meetings   118–19
sign language   48–9, 51
social care, defining   4
Social Care Association   6, 8, 12, 15, 77
   on supervision   106
social justice   16, 140
social welfare   16
Sowa, Theo   97
staff ratios   106
Stevenson, O.   19
summary needs profile   66
supervision   106, 134–7
symbolic communication   46–8, 51

task-centred work   84–5, 86, 110
team meetings   116, 117–20
teamwork   103–4, 105, 113, 114, 116–20
   advantages of   120
   and anti-discriminatory practice   28–9, 118
   and co-keyworking   121
terminal illness   91
therapeutic crisis intervention   84, 111
Thompson, Neil   25
Thomson, H.   1, 24, 48, 64, 134
thoughts and feelings, behavioural work
      on   72–4
three stage skills model of counselling   56,
      59–60
time, constructive use of   104–5
   and team meetings   119
touch, showing warmth through   54
Townsend, P.   37

training   106–7
Treillion, S.   113
Tuckman, B.W.   94, 96, 97
Tyn-y-Pwll residential project   49–50

unconditional positive regard   53–4, 58, 59

values   2, 15–17
   and assessment   64, 65
   and counselling   56, 57
   influence on practice   136
verbal communication   46–8, 51, 53
violence, right to protection from   2, 18–19,
      28
vocation   46, 47

Wagner Committee   111
Wagner, G.   15
Ward, A.   113, 134, 137
Waterside Education and Training   28–9, 30
Wheal, A.   5, 9, 45, 67
Where there's a will (Video Arts film)   104
Willmott, P.   36
Wineman, D.   110
Wolfensberger, W.   12
Worden, J.W.   138

Young, M.   36
young offenders, intermediate treatment
      project   97
young people
   choice and risk taking   20
   and social carer's tasks   5, 9
   and the Tyn-y-Pwll residential
      project   49–50